STAR WARS®

EWOKS

SHADOWS OF ENDOR

DESIGNER JIMMY PRESLER

ASSISTANT EDITOR FREDDYE LINS

EDITOR DAVE MARSHALL

PRESIDENT & PUBLISHER MIKE RICHARDSON

Special thanks to Joanne Chan Taylor, Leland Chee, Troy Alders, Carol Roeder, Jann Moorhead, and David Anderman at Lucas Licensing.

STAR WARS: EWOKS—SHADOWS OF ENDOR

Published by Dark Horse Books
A division of Dark Horse Comics, Inc.
10956 SE Main Street
Milwaukie, OR 97222

DarkHorse.com | StarWars.com

International Licensing: (503) 905-2377
To find a comics shop in your area, call the Comic Shop Locator Service toll-free at 1-888-266-4226.

Library of Congress Cataloging-in-Publication Data

Giallongo, Zack, 1979-
 Star Wars, ewoks : shadows of Endor / story & art, Zack Giallongo ; colors, Braden Lamb ; lettering, Michael Heisler ; cover art, Zack Giallongo with Braden Lamb. -- First edition.
     pages cm
 Summary: "Finding a neighboring tribe of Duloks has been enslaved by the Empire, and a legendary beast has been awakened, the peaceful Ewoks prepare to deal with two powerful foes"-- Provided by publisher.
 ISBN 978-1-61655-174-2
1. Graphic novels. [1. Graphic novels. 2. Science fiction.] I. Lamb, Braden, illustrator. II. Title. III. Title: Ewoks, shadows of Endor. IV. Title: Shadows of Endor.
 PZ7.7.G52St 2013
 741.5'315--dc23
                                              2013017398

First edition: October 2013
ISBN 978-1-61655-174-2

10 9 8 7 6 5 4 3 2 1
Printed in China

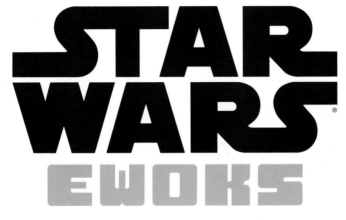

SHADOWS OF ENDOR

STORY & ART ZACK GIALLONGO

COLORS BRADEN LAMB

LETTERING MICHAEL HEISLER

COVER ART ZACK GIALLONGO WITH BRADEN LAMB

THE REBELLION
FROM THE BATTLE OF YAVIN TO FIVE YEARS AFTER

Open resistance begins to spread across the galaxy in protest of the Empire's tyranny. Rebel groups unite, and the Galactic Civil War begins. This era starts with the Rebel victory that secured the Death Star plans, and ends a year after the death of the Emperor high over the forest moon of Endor. This is the era in which the events in *A New Hope*, *The Empire Strikes Back*, and *Return of the Jedi* take place.

The events in this story take place shortly before the events in *Star Wars*: Episode VI—*Return of the Jedi*.

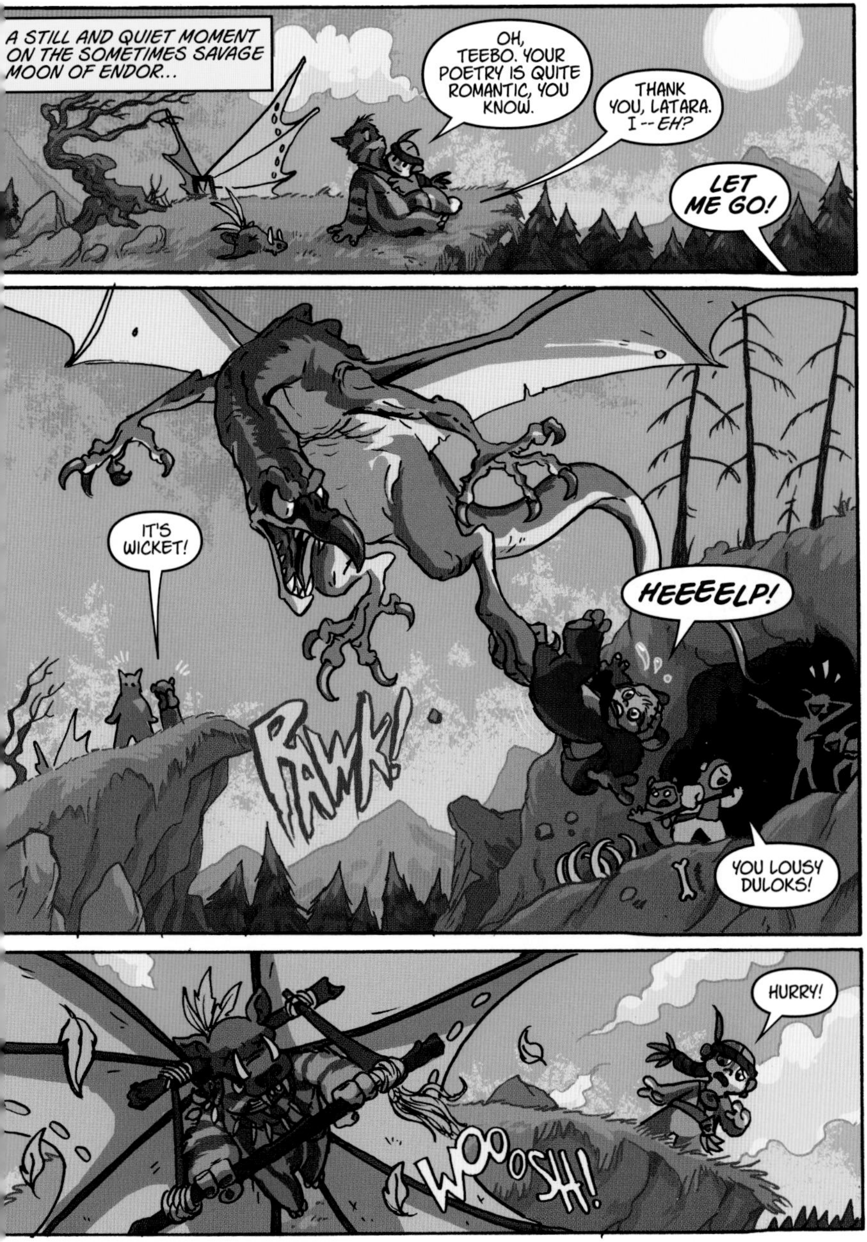

A STILL AND QUIET MOMENT ON THE SOMETIMES SAVAGE MOON OF ENDOR...
OH, TEEBO. YOUR POETRY IS QUITE ROMANTIC, YOU KNOW.
THANK YOU, LATARA. I -- EH?
LET ME GO!
IT'S WICKET!
HEEEELP!
RAWK!
YOU LOUSY DULOKS!
HURRY!
WOOOOSH!

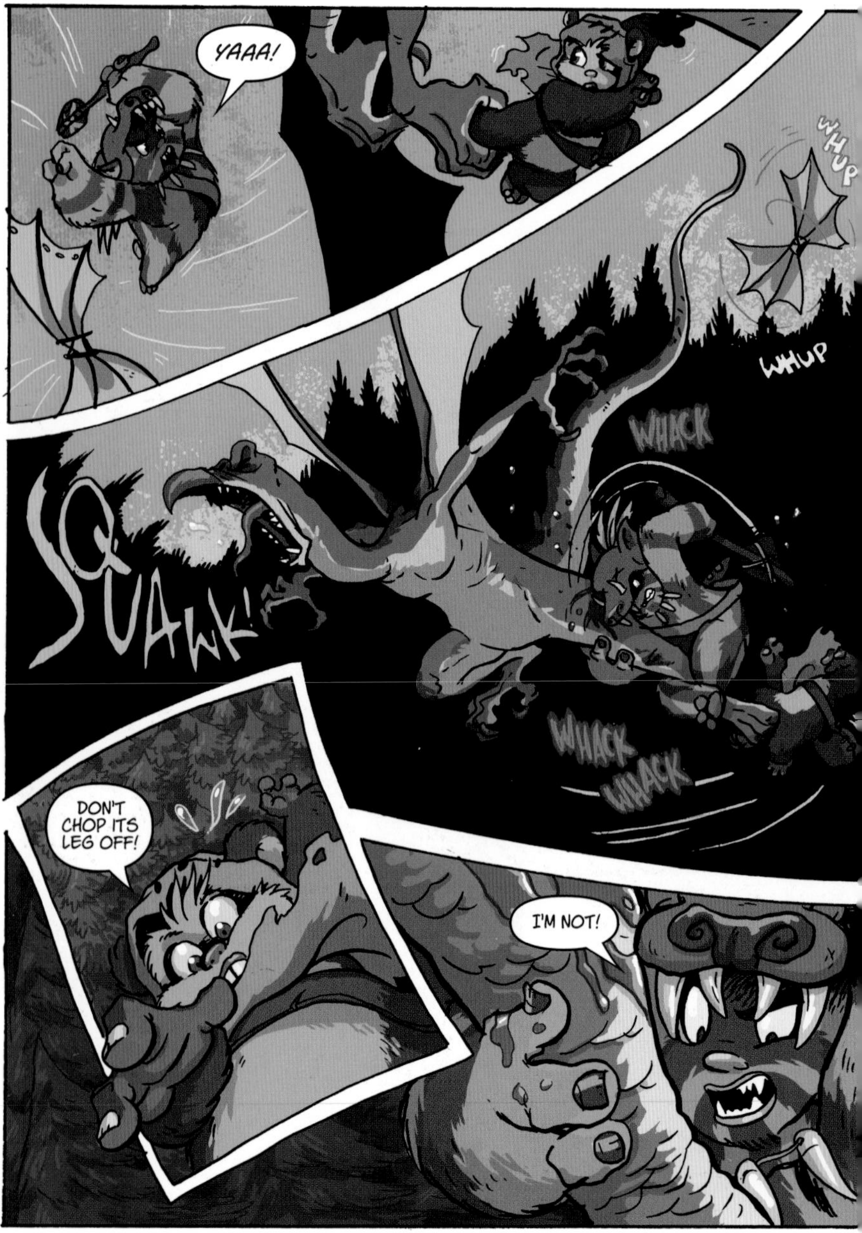
YAAA!
WHUP
WHUP
WHACK
SQUAWK!
WHACK
WHACK
DON'T CHOP ITS LEG OFF!
I'M NOT!

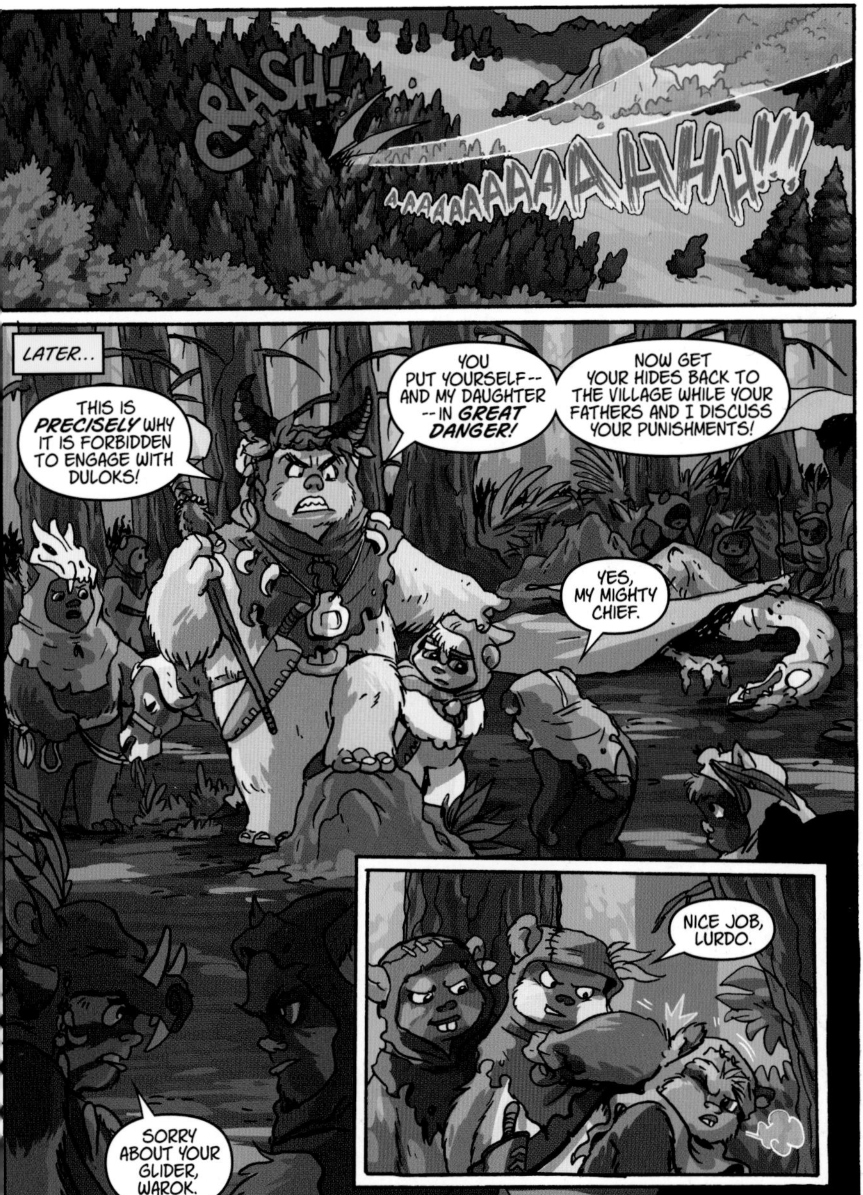
CRASH!
AAAAAAAAAAHHH!!
LATER...
THIS IS *PRECISELY* WHY IT IS FORBIDDEN TO ENGAGE WITH DULOKS!
YOU PUT YOURSELF-- AND MY DAUGHTER --IN *GREAT DANGER!*
NOW GET YOUR HIDES BACK TO THE VILLAGE WHILE YOUR FATHERS AND I DISCUSS YOUR PUNISHMENTS!
YES, MY MIGHTY CHIEF.
SORRY ABOUT YOUR GLIDER, WAROK.
NICE JOB, LURDO.

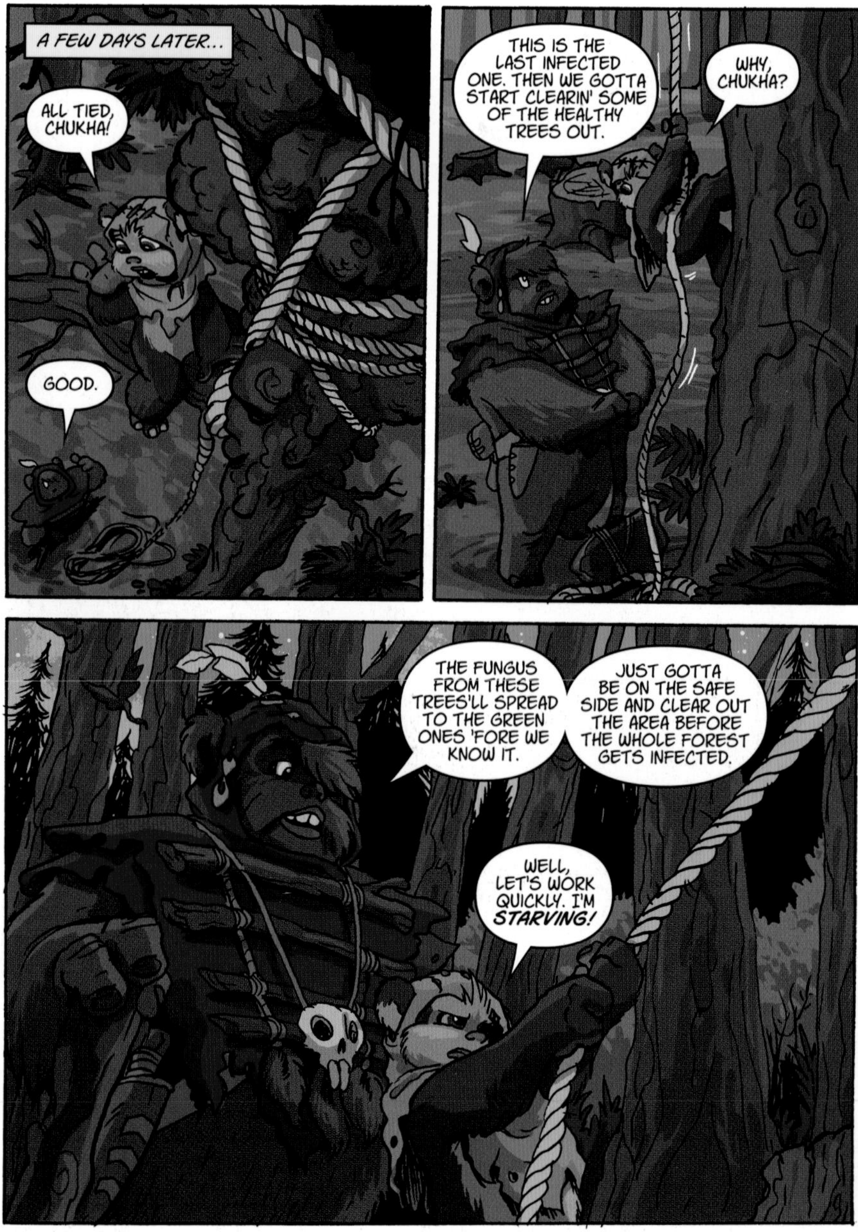
A FEW DAYS LATER...
ALL TIED, CHUKHA!
GOOD.
THIS IS THE LAST INFECTED ONE. THEN WE GOTTA START CLEARIN' SOME OF THE HEALTHY TREES OUT.
WHY, CHUKHA?
THE FUNGUS FROM THESE TREES'LL SPREAD TO THE GREEN ONES 'FORE WE KNOW IT.
JUST GOTTA BE ON THE SAFE SIDE AND CLEAR OUT THE AREA BEFORE THE WHOLE FOREST GETS INFECTED.
WELL, LET'S WORK QUICKLY. I'M STARVING!

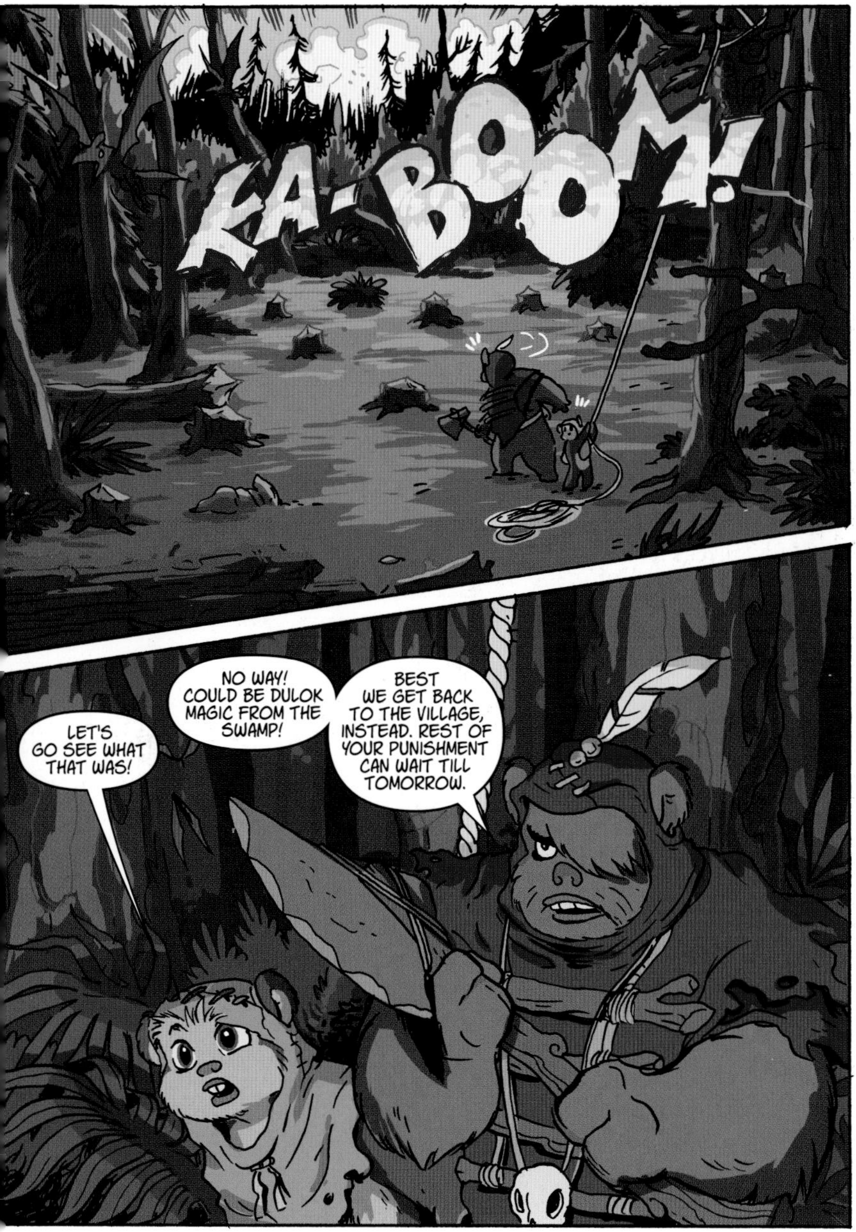
KA-BOOM!
LET'S GO SEE WHAT THAT WAS!
NO WAY! COULD BE DULOK MAGIC FROM THE SWAMP!
BEST WE GET BACK TO THE VILLAGE, INSTEAD. REST OF YOUR PUNISHMENT CAN WAIT TILL TOMORROW.

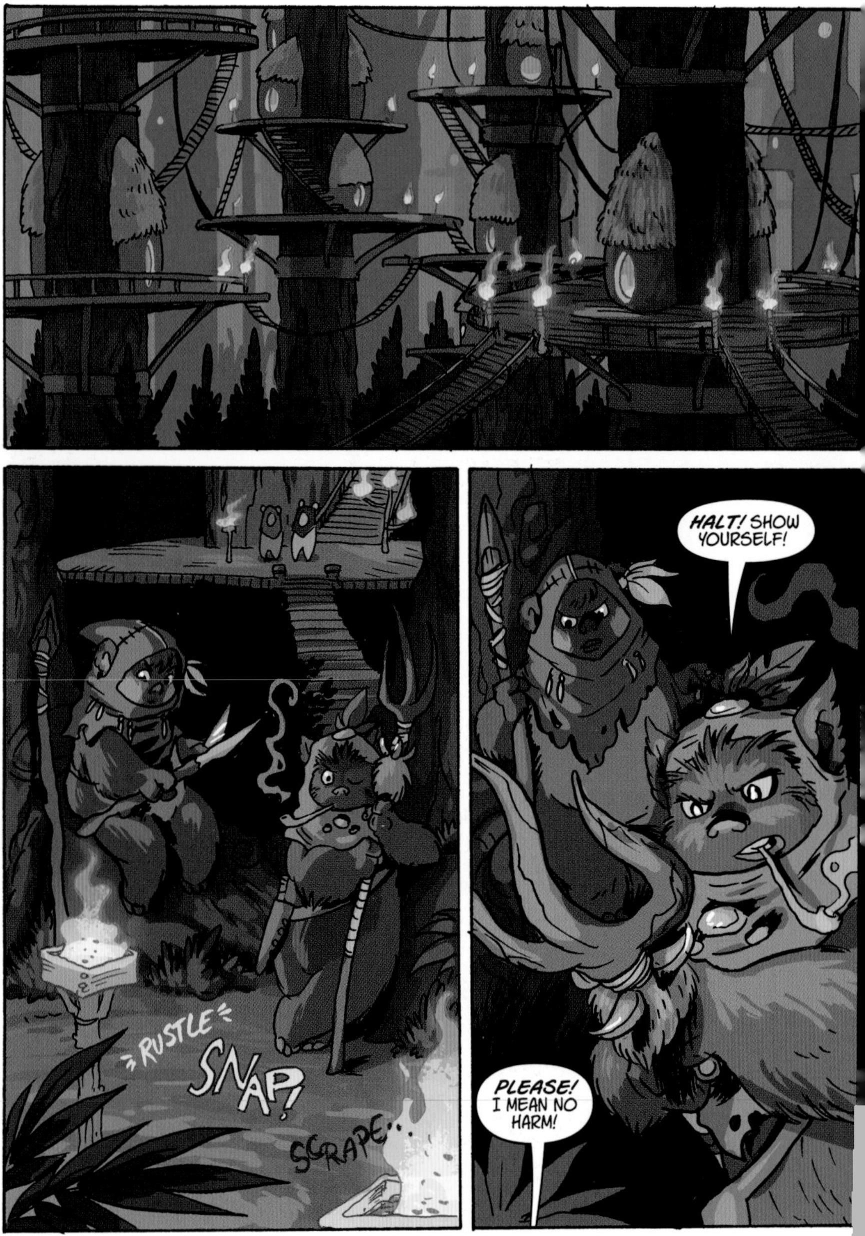
RUSTLE
SNAP!
SCRAPE
HALT! SHOW YOURSELF!
PLEASE! I MEAN NO HARM!

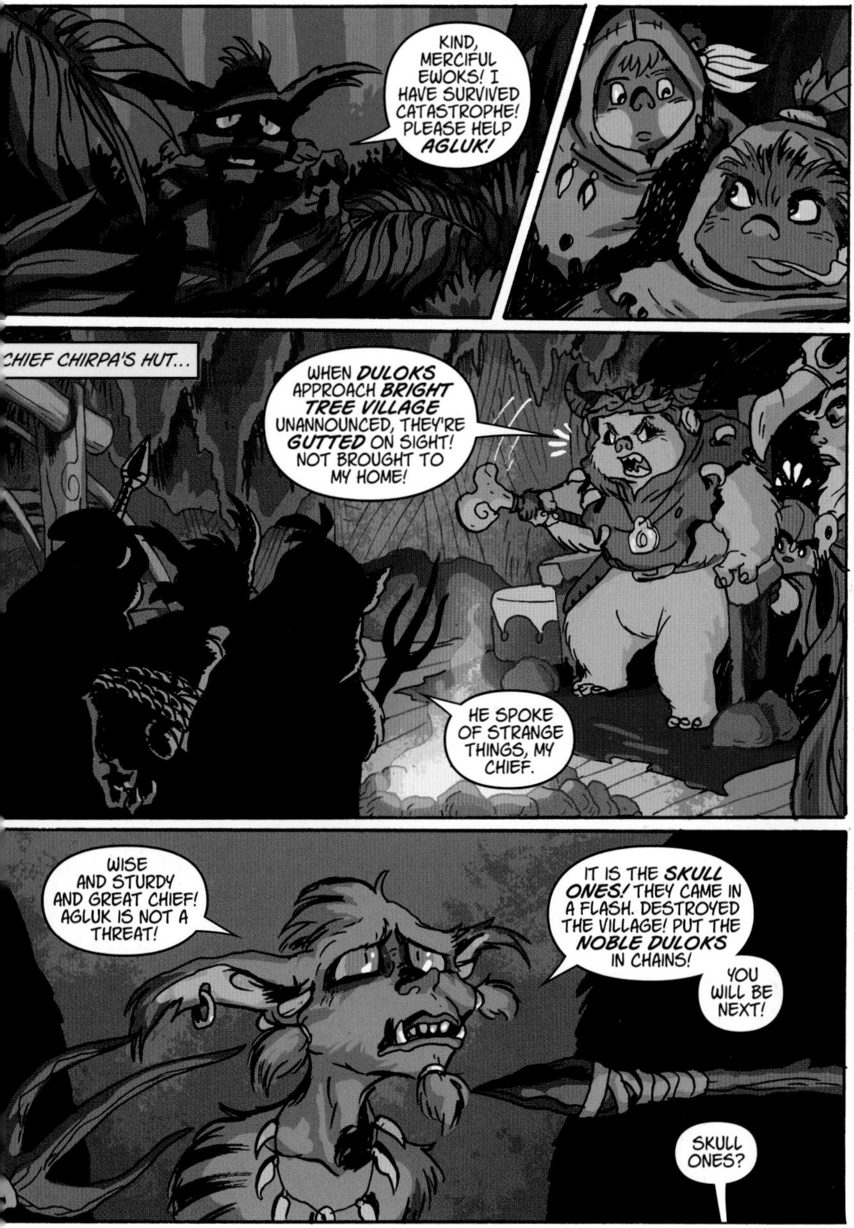
KIND, MERCIFUL EWOKS! I HAVE SURVIVED CATASTROPHE! PLEASE HELP AGLUK!
CHIEF CHIRPA'S HUT...
WHEN DULOKS APPROACH BRIGHT TREE VILLAGE UNANNOUNCED, THEY'RE GUTTED ON SIGHT! NOT BROUGHT TO MY HOME!
HE SPOKE OF STRANGE THINGS, MY CHIEF.
WISE AND STURDY AND GREAT CHIEF! AGLUK IS NOT A THREAT!
IT IS THE SKULL ONES! THEY CAME IN A FLASH. DESTROYED THE VILLAGE! PUT THE NOBLE DULOKS IN CHAINS!
YOU WILL BE NEXT!
SKULL ONES?

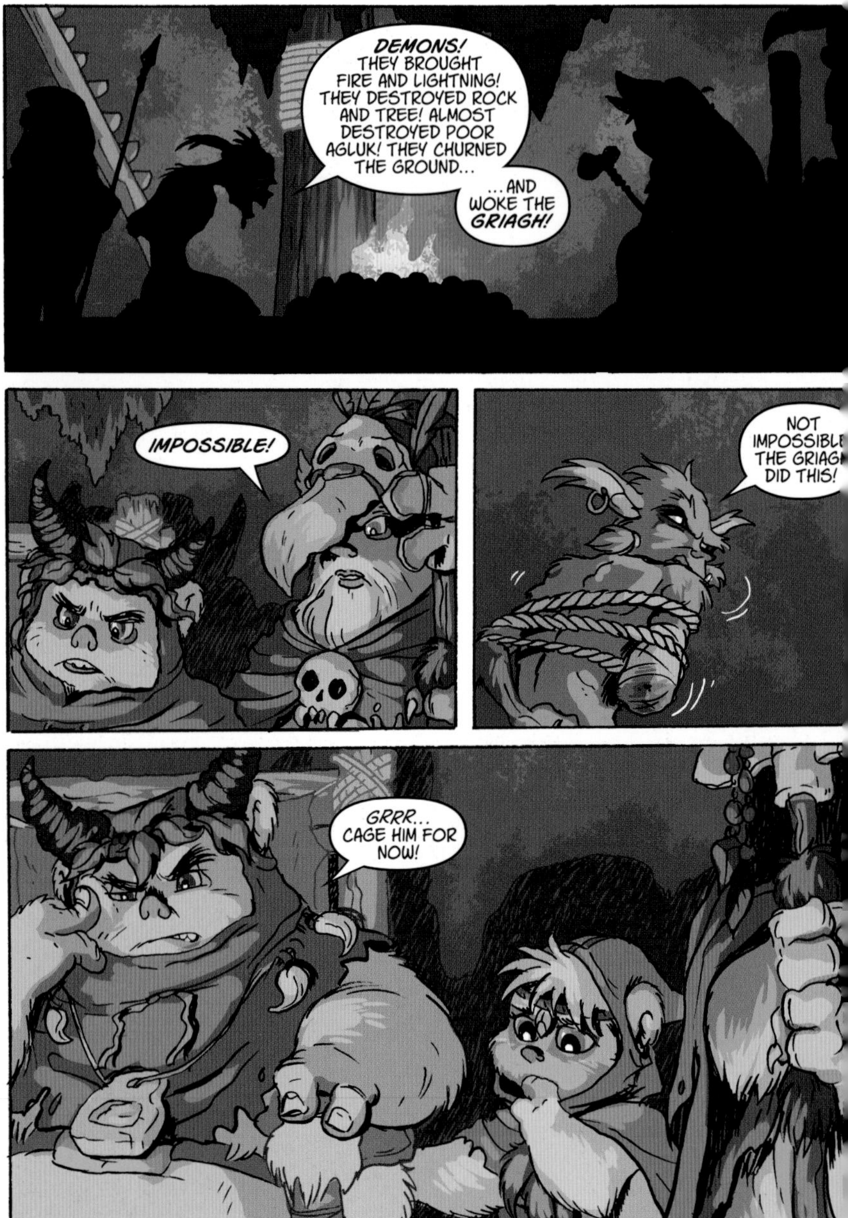
DEMONS! THEY BROUGHT FIRE AND LIGHTNING! THEY DESTROYED ROCK AND TREE! ALMOST DESTROYED POOR AGLUK! THEY CHURNED THE GROUND...
...AND WOKE THE GRIAGH!
IMPOSSIBLE!
NOT IMPOSSIBL THE GRIAG DID THIS!
GRRR... CAGE HIM FOR NOW!

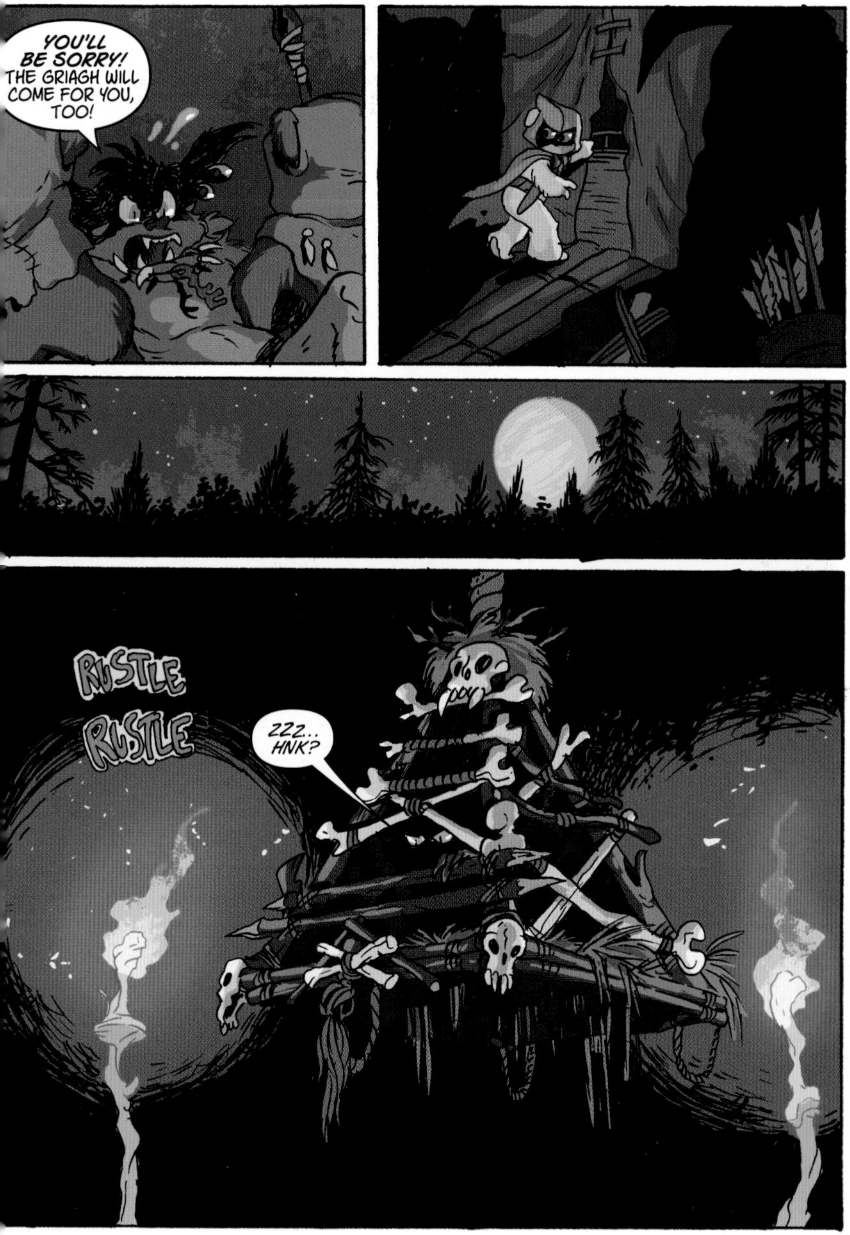
YOU'LL BE SORRY! THE GRIAGH WILL COME FOR YOU, TOO!
RUSTLE
RUSTLE
ZZZ... HNK?

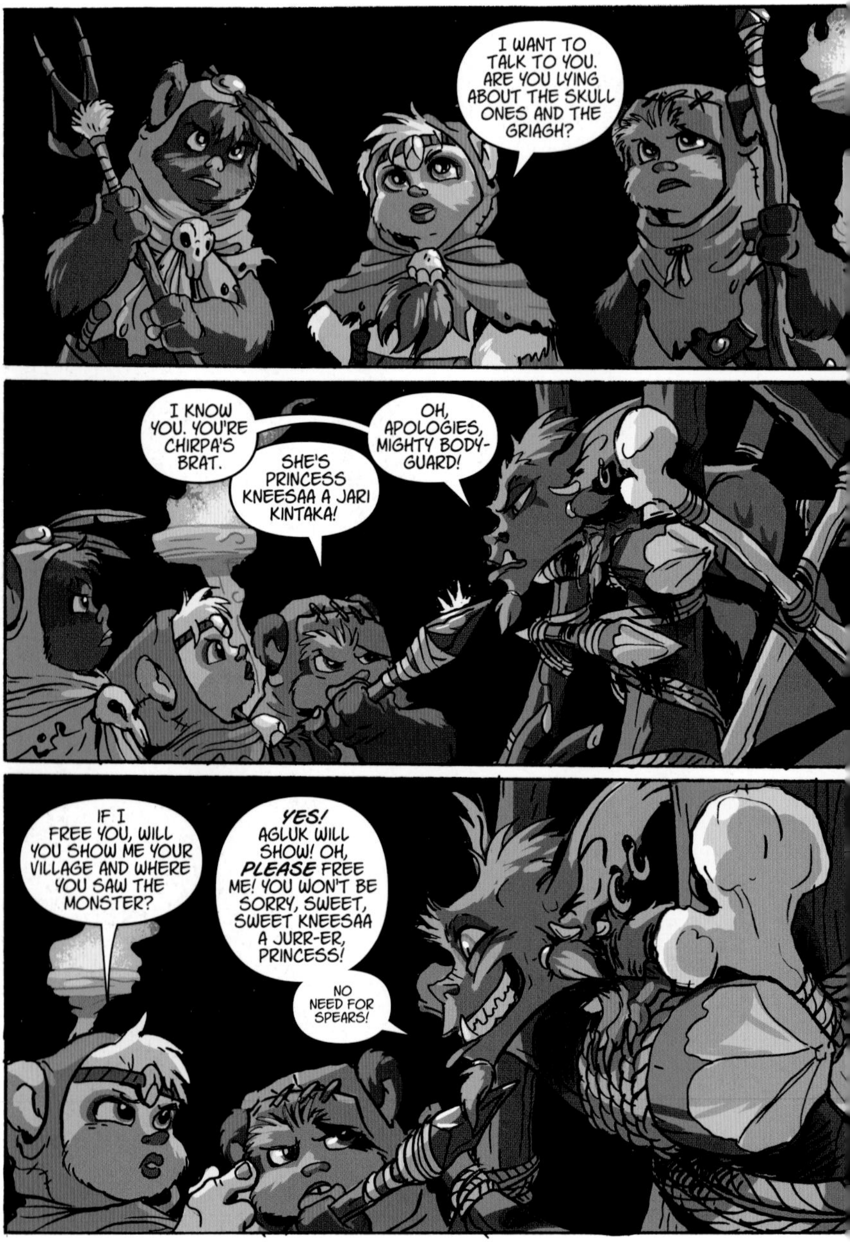
I WANT TO TALK TO YOU. ARE YOU LYING ABOUT THE SKULL ONES AND THE GRIAGH?
I KNOW YOU. YOU'RE CHIRPA'S BRAT.
OH, APOLOGIES, MIGHTY BODY-GUARD!
SHE'S PRINCESS KNEESAA A JARI KINTAKA!
IF I FREE YOU, WILL YOU SHOW ME YOUR VILLAGE AND WHERE YOU SAW THE MONSTER?
YES! AGLUK WILL SHOW! OH, PLEASE FREE ME! YOU WON'T BE SORRY, SWEET, SWEET KNEESAA A JURR-ER, PRINCESS!
NO NEED FOR SPEARS!

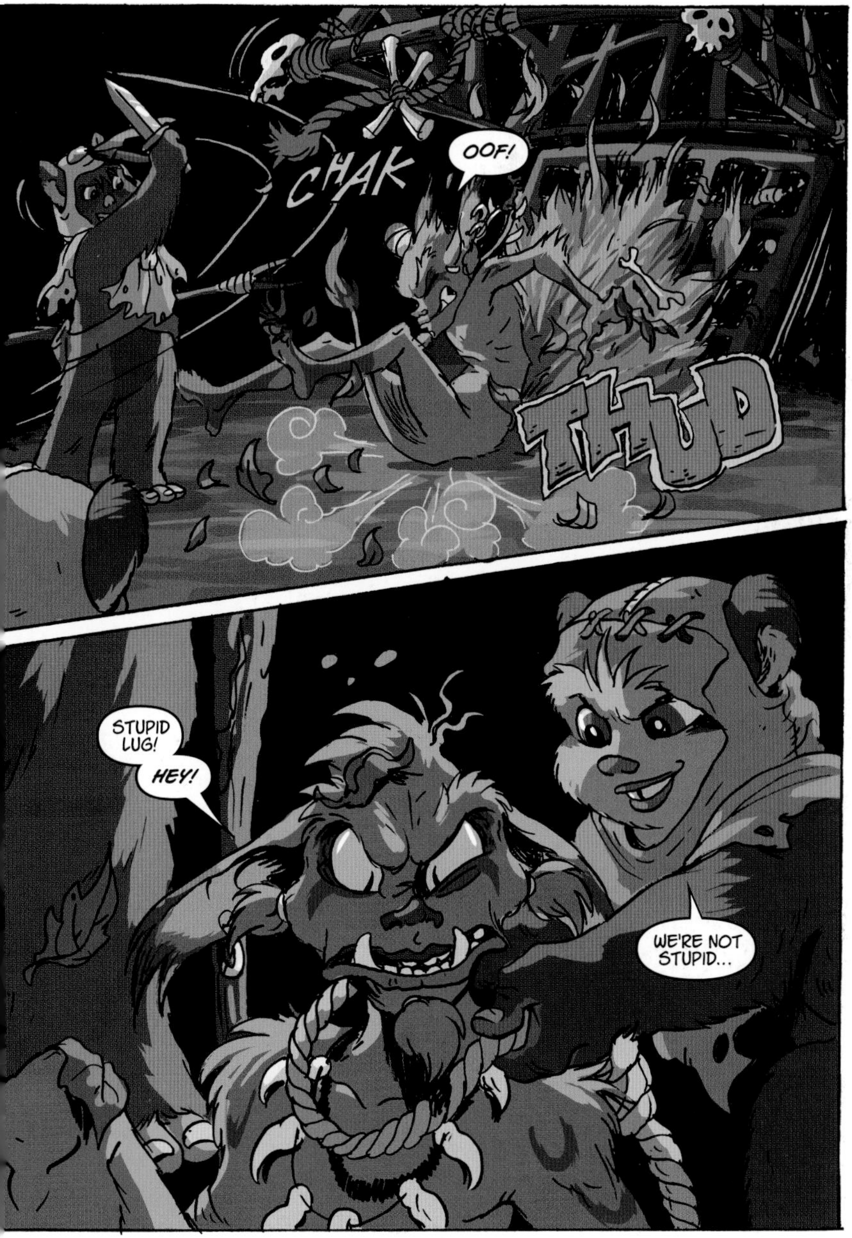
CHAK
OOF!
THUD
STUPID LUG!
HEY!
WE'RE NOT STUPID...

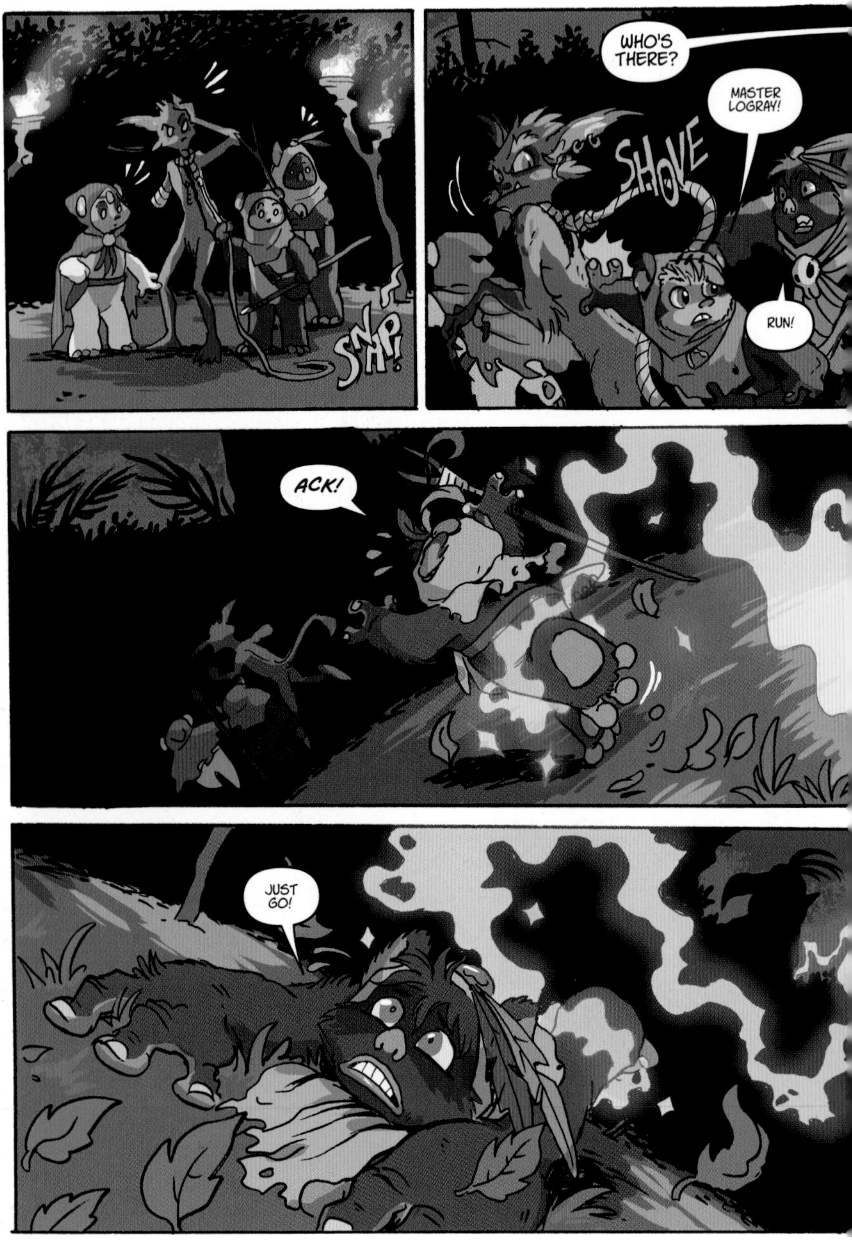
SNAP!
WHO'S THERE?
SHOVE
MASTER LOGRAY!
RUN!
ACK!
JUST GO!

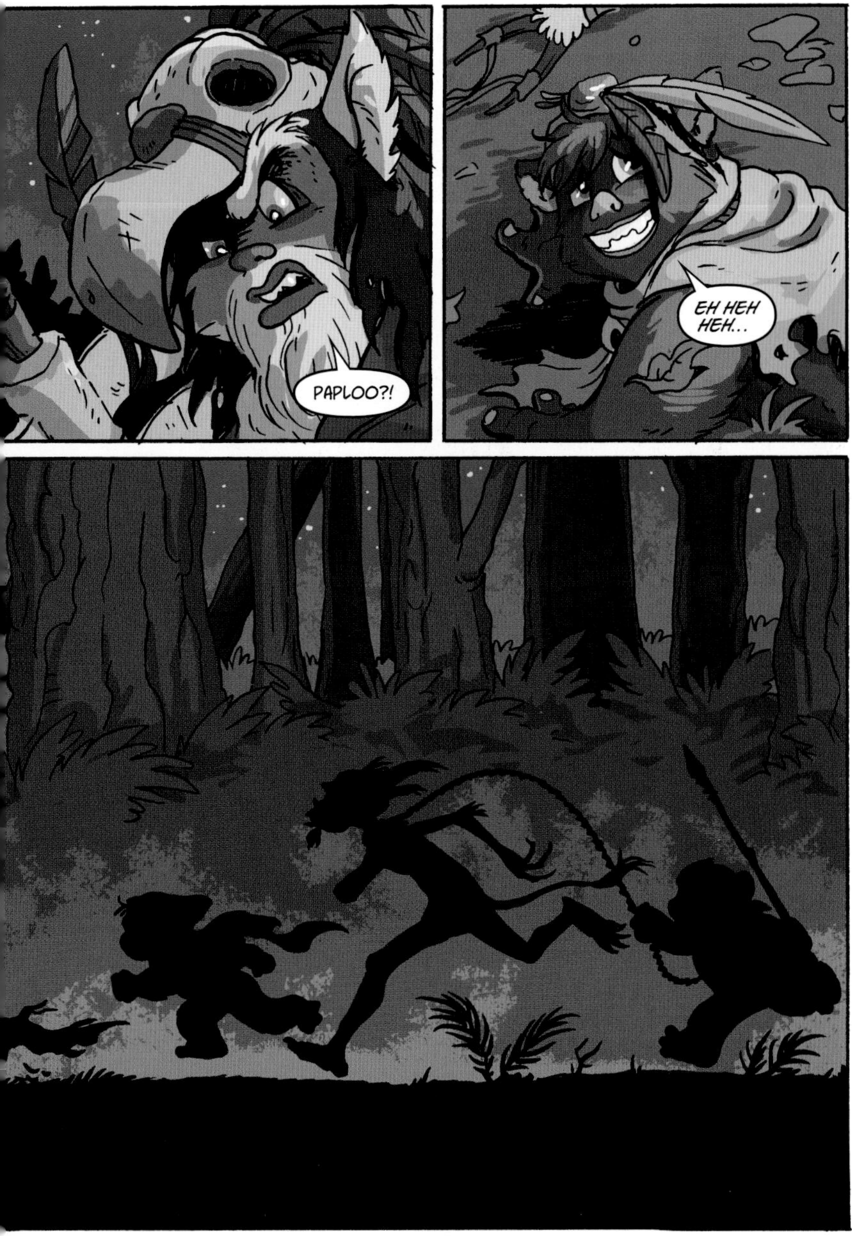
PAPLOO?!
EH HEH HEH...

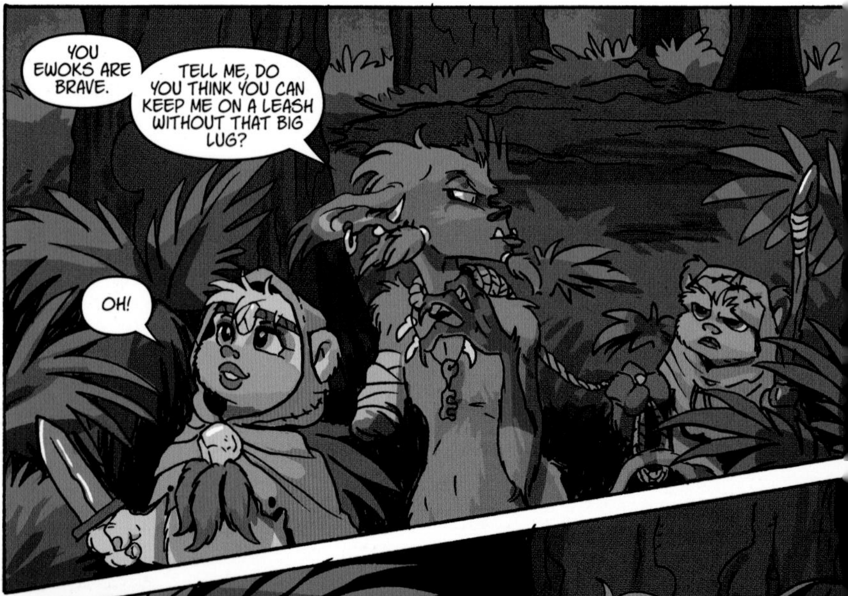
YOU EWOKS ARE BRAVE.
TELL ME, DO YOU THINK YOU CAN KEEP ME ON A LEASH WITHOUT THAT BIG LUG?
OH!

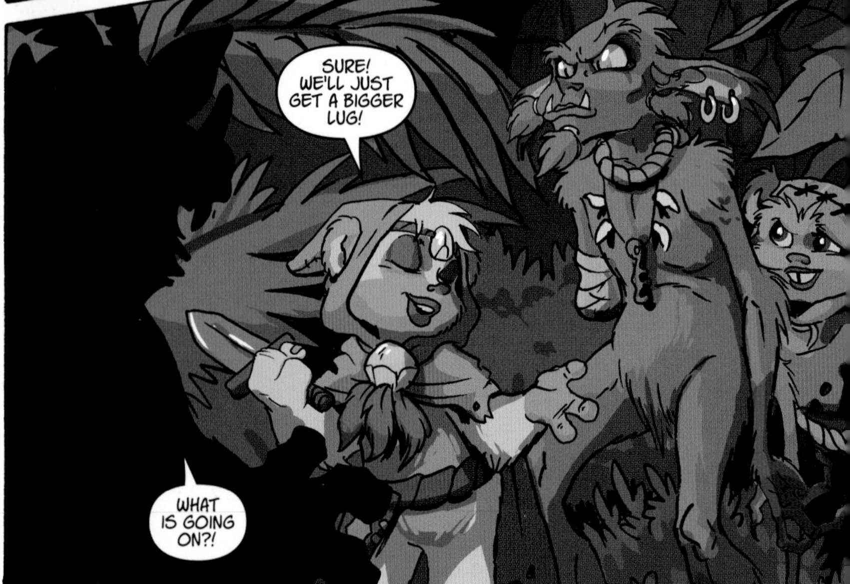
SURE! WE'LL JUST GET A BIGGER LUG!
WHAT IS GOING ON?!

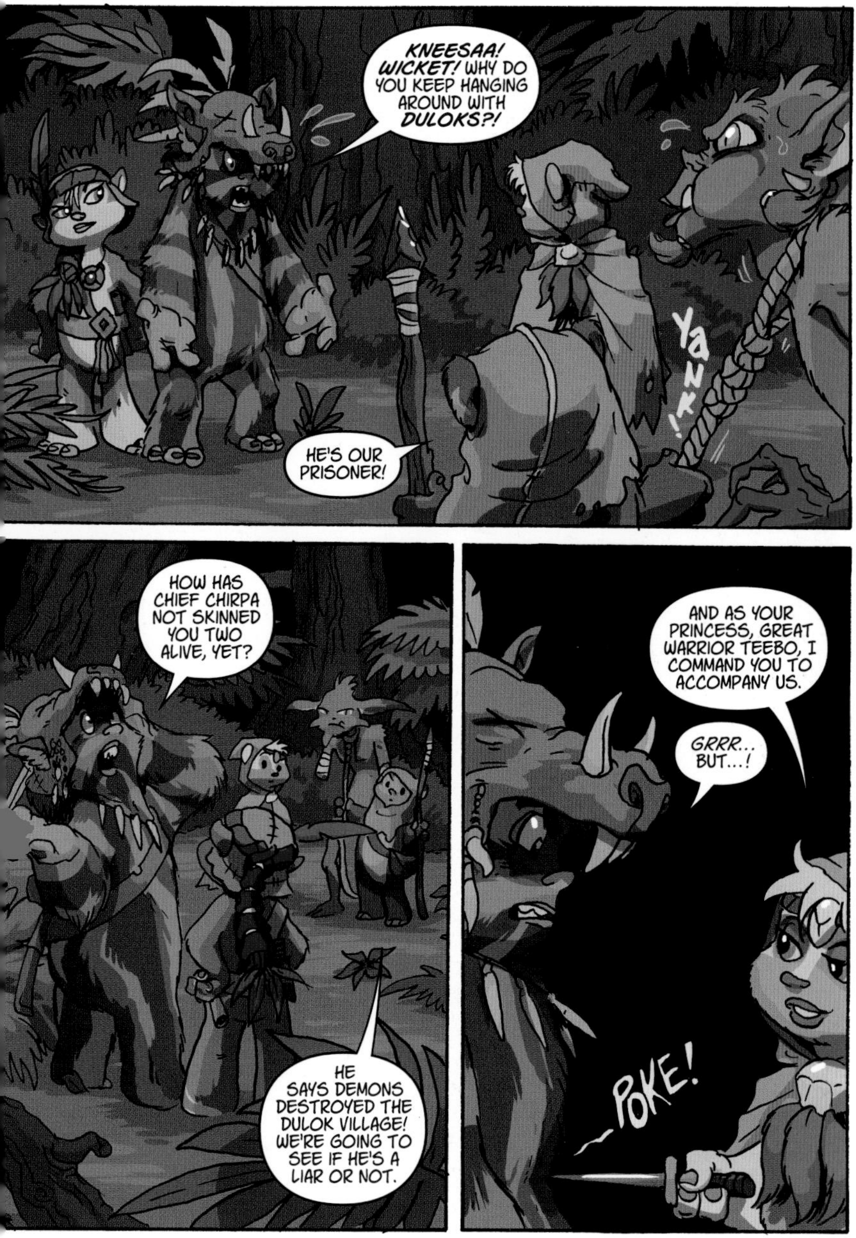
KNEESAA! WICKET! WHY DO YOU KEEP HANGING AROUND WITH DULOKS?!
YANK!
HE'S OUR PRISONER!
HOW HAS CHIEF CHIRPA NOT SKINNED YOU TWO ALIVE, YET?
HE SAYS DEMONS DESTROYED THE DULOK VILLAGE! WE'RE GOING TO SEE IF HE'S A LIAR OR NOT.
AND AS YOUR PRINCESS, GREAT WARRIOR TEEBO, I COMMAND YOU TO ACCOMPANY US.
GRRR... BUT...!
POKE!

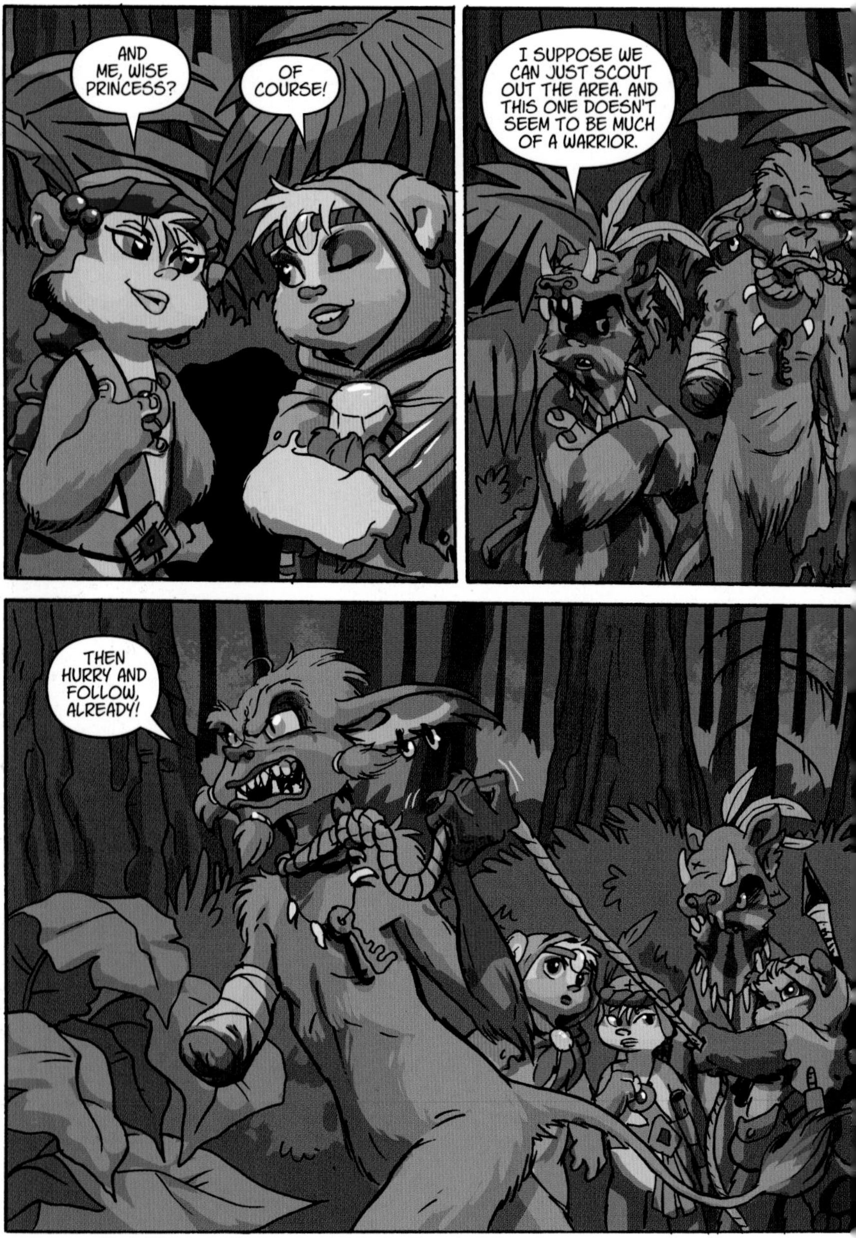
AND ME, WISE PRINCESS?
OF COURSE!
I SUPPOSE WE CAN JUST SCOUT OUT THE AREA. AND THIS ONE DOESN'T SEEM TO BE MUCH OF A WARRIOR.
THEN HURRY AND FOLLOW, ALREADY!

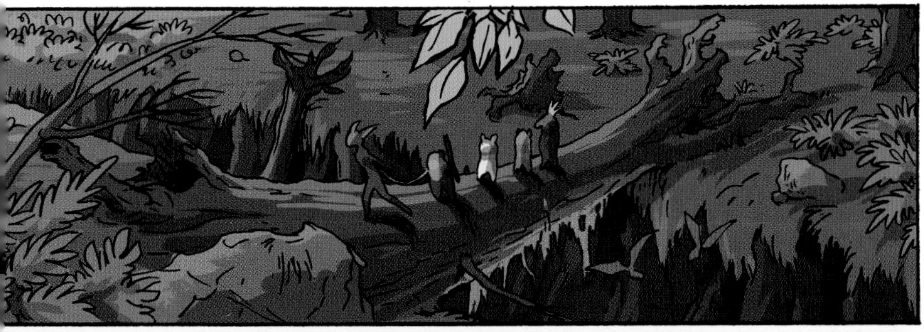

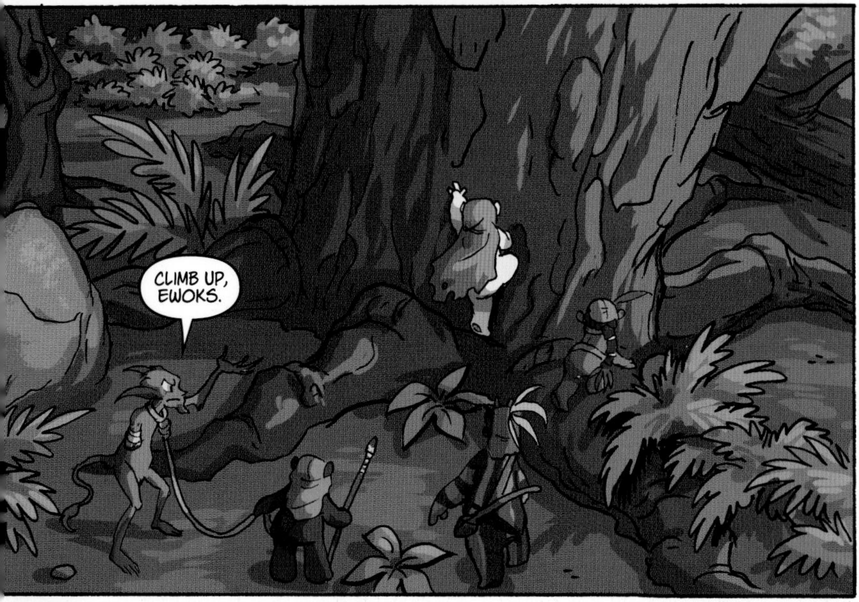

CLIMB UP, EWOKS.

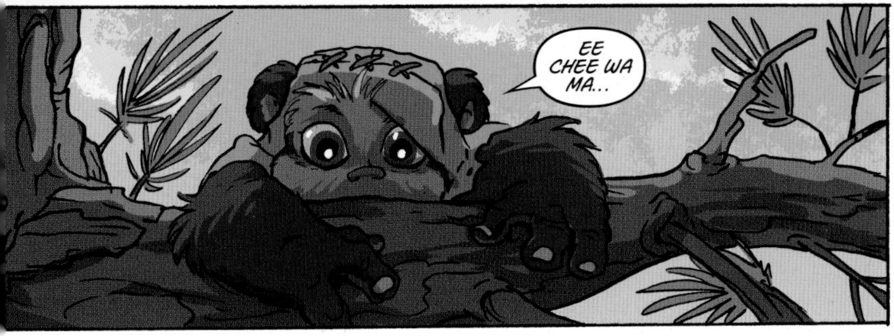

EE CHEE WA MA...

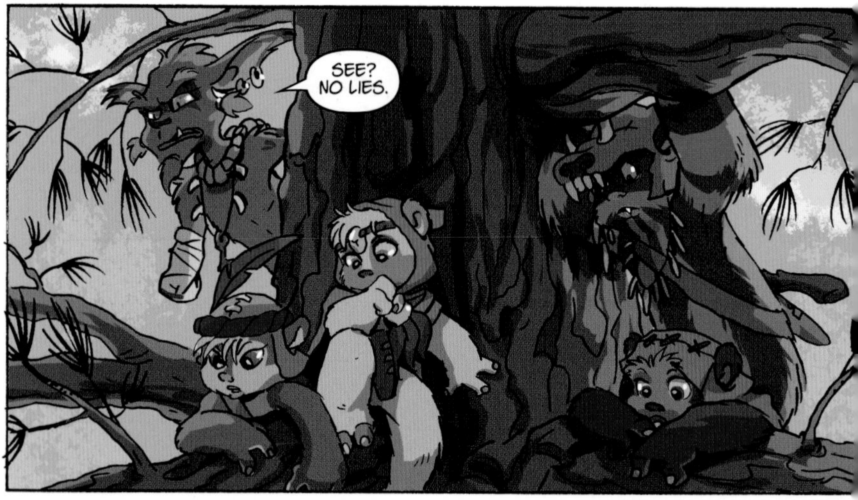
SEE? NO LIES.

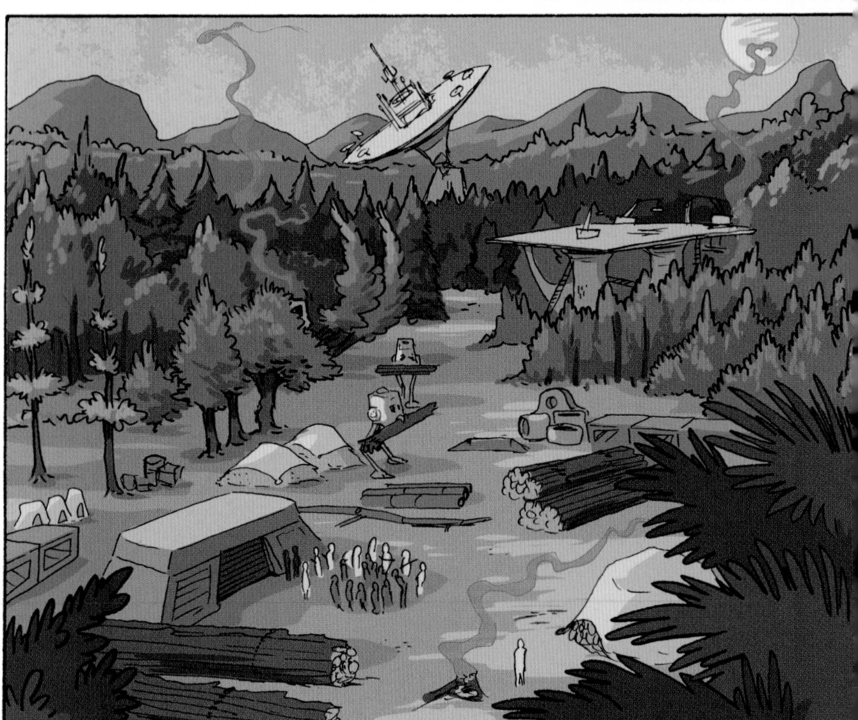

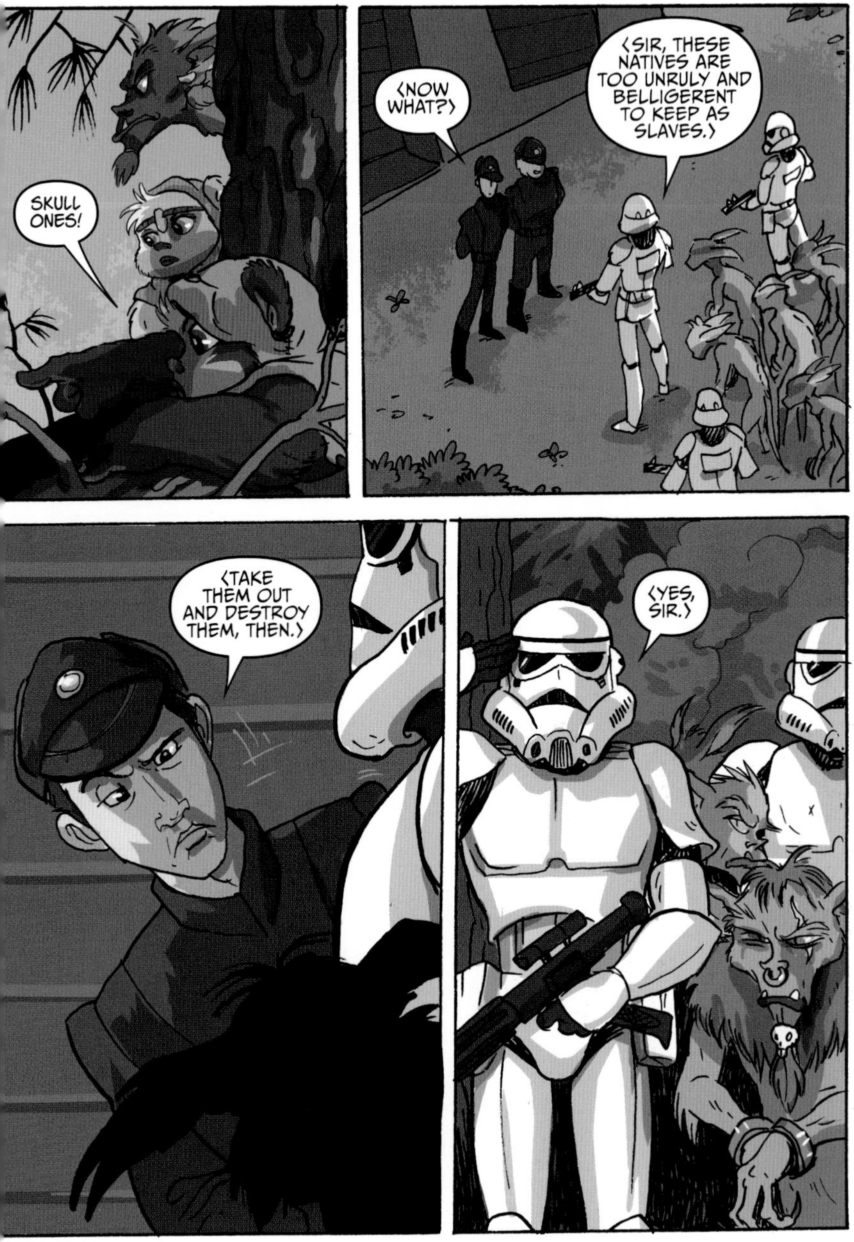
SKULL ONES!
‹NOW WHAT?›
‹SIR, THESE NATIVES ARE TOO UNRULY AND BELLIGERENT TO KEEP AS SLAVES.›
‹TAKE THEM OUT AND DESTROY THEM, THEN.›
‹YES, SIR.›

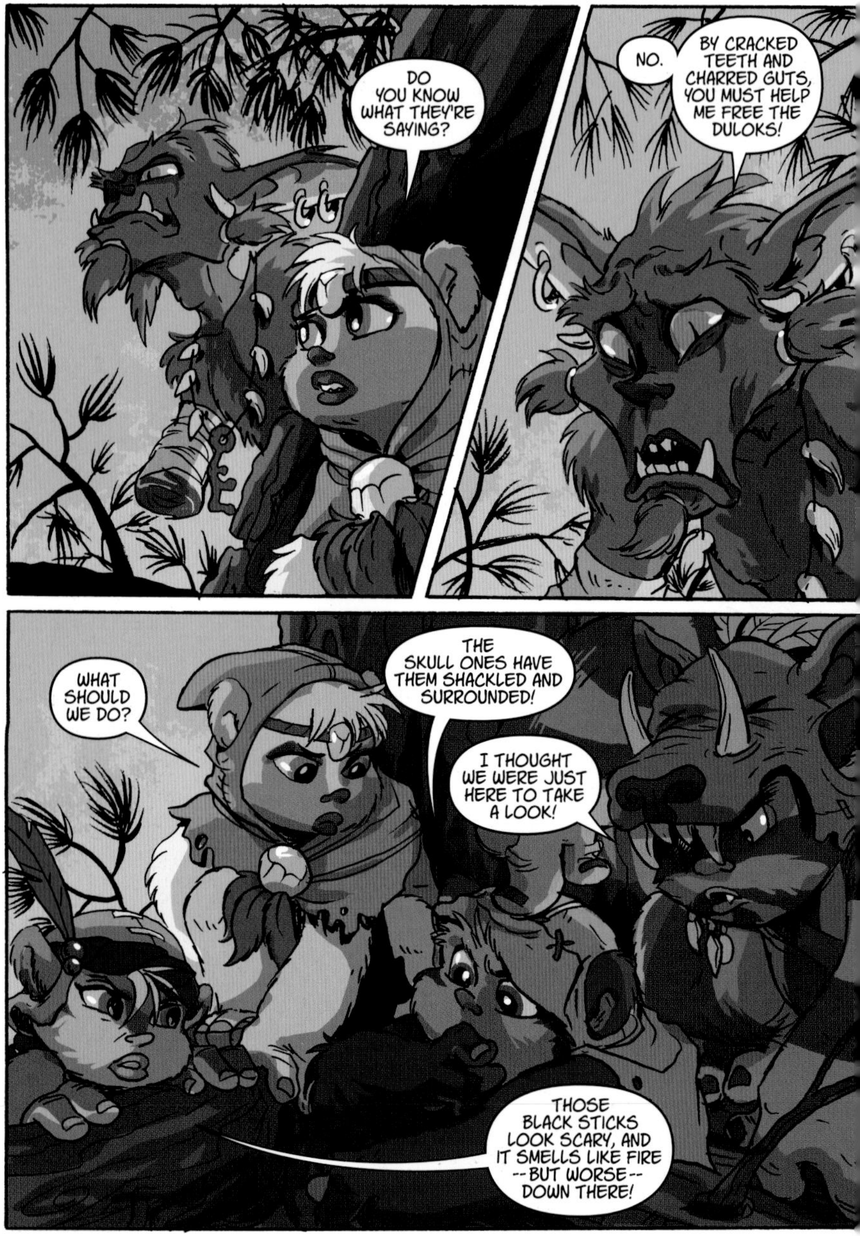
DO YOU KNOW WHAT THEY'RE SAYING?
NO.
BY CRACKED TEETH AND CHARRED GUTS, YOU MUST HELP ME FREE THE DULOKS!
WHAT SHOULD WE DO?
THE SKULL ONES HAVE THEM SHACKLED AND SURROUNDED!
I THOUGHT WE WERE JUST HERE TO TAKE A LOOK!
THOSE BLACK STICKS LOOK SCARY, AND IT SMELLS LIKE FIRE --BUT WORSE-- DOWN THERE!

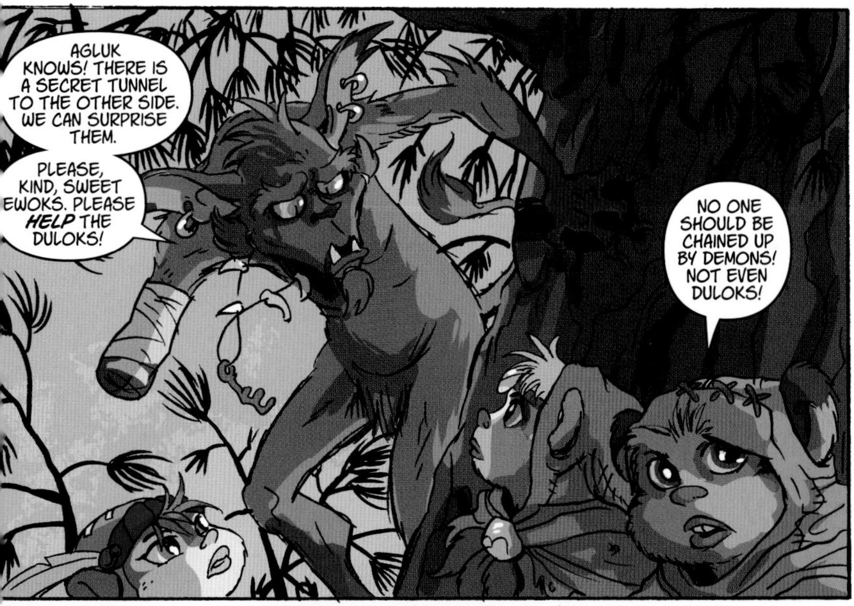
AGLUK KNOWS! THERE IS A SECRET TUNNEL TO THE OTHER SIDE. WE CAN SURPRISE THEM.
PLEASE, KIND, SWEET EWOKS. PLEASE *HELP* THE DULOKS!
NO ONE SHOULD BE CHAINED UP BY DEMONS! NOT EVEN DULOKS!

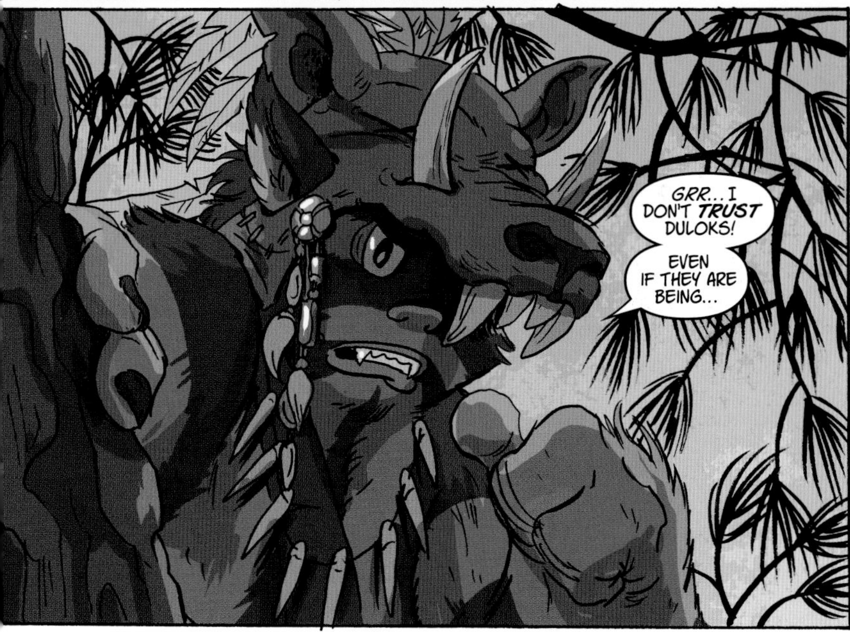
GRR... I DON'T *TRUST* DULOKS!
EVEN IF THEY ARE BEING...

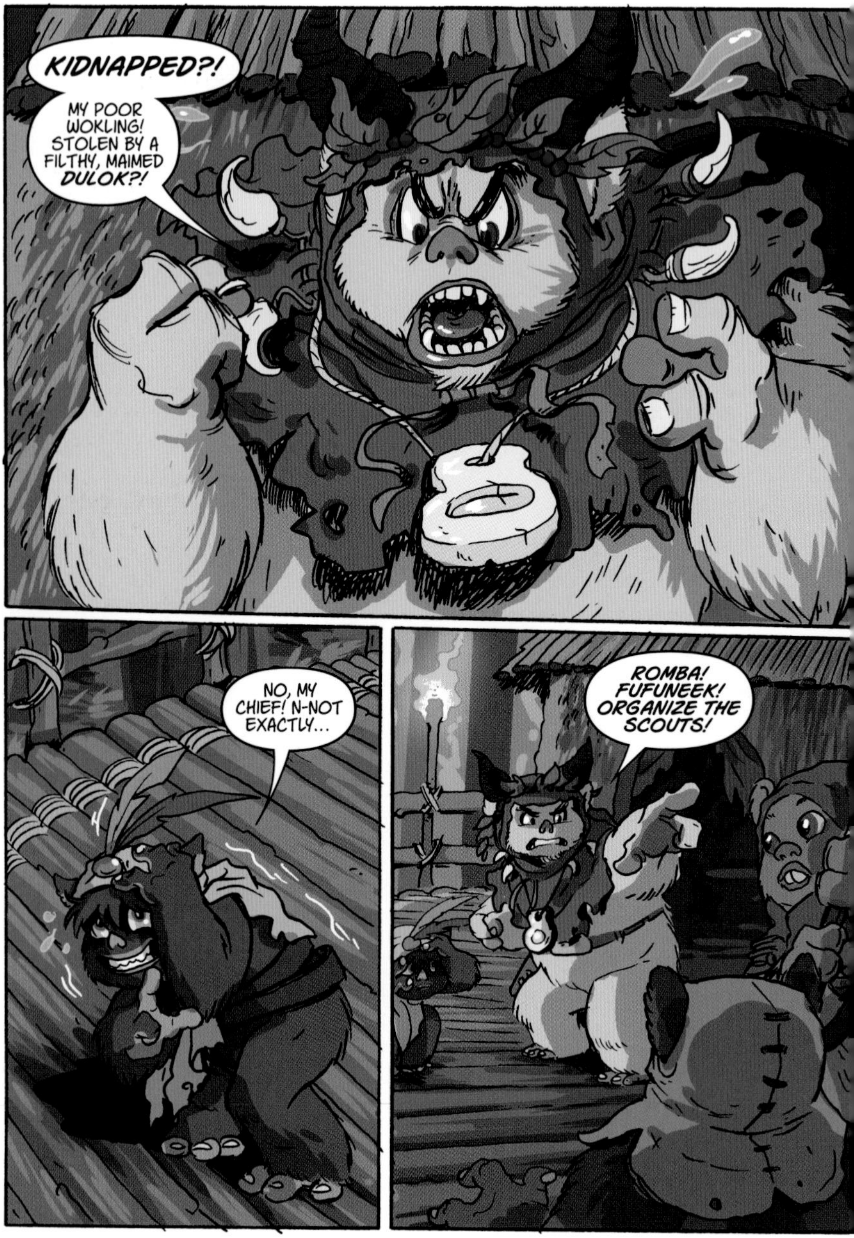
KIDNAPPED?!
MY POOR WOKLING! STOLEN BY A FILTHY, MAIMED DULOK?!
NO, MY CHIEF! N-NOT EXACTLY...
ROMBA! FUFUNEEK! ORGANIZE THE SCOUTS!

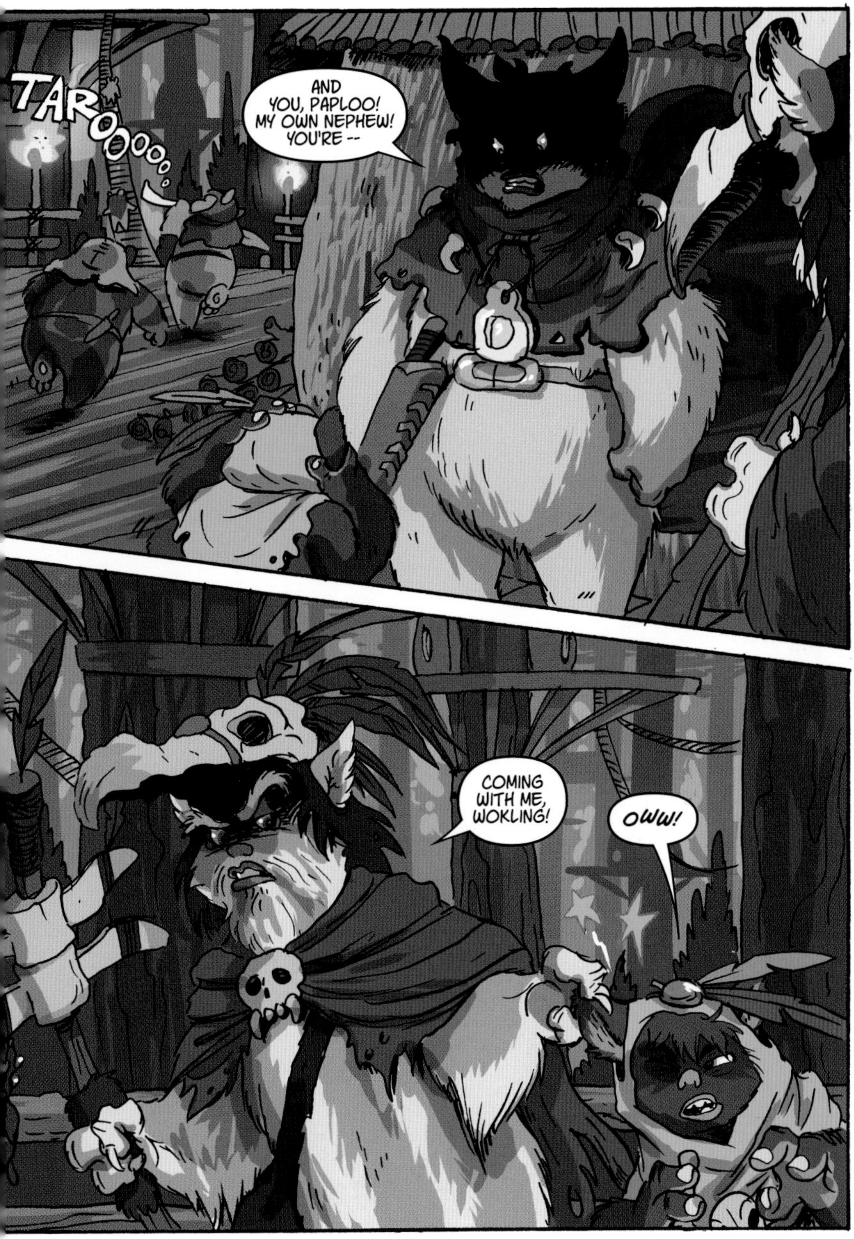
TAROOOOOO
AND YOU, PAPLOO! MY OWN NEPHEW! YOU'RE --
COMING WITH ME, WOKLING!
OWW!

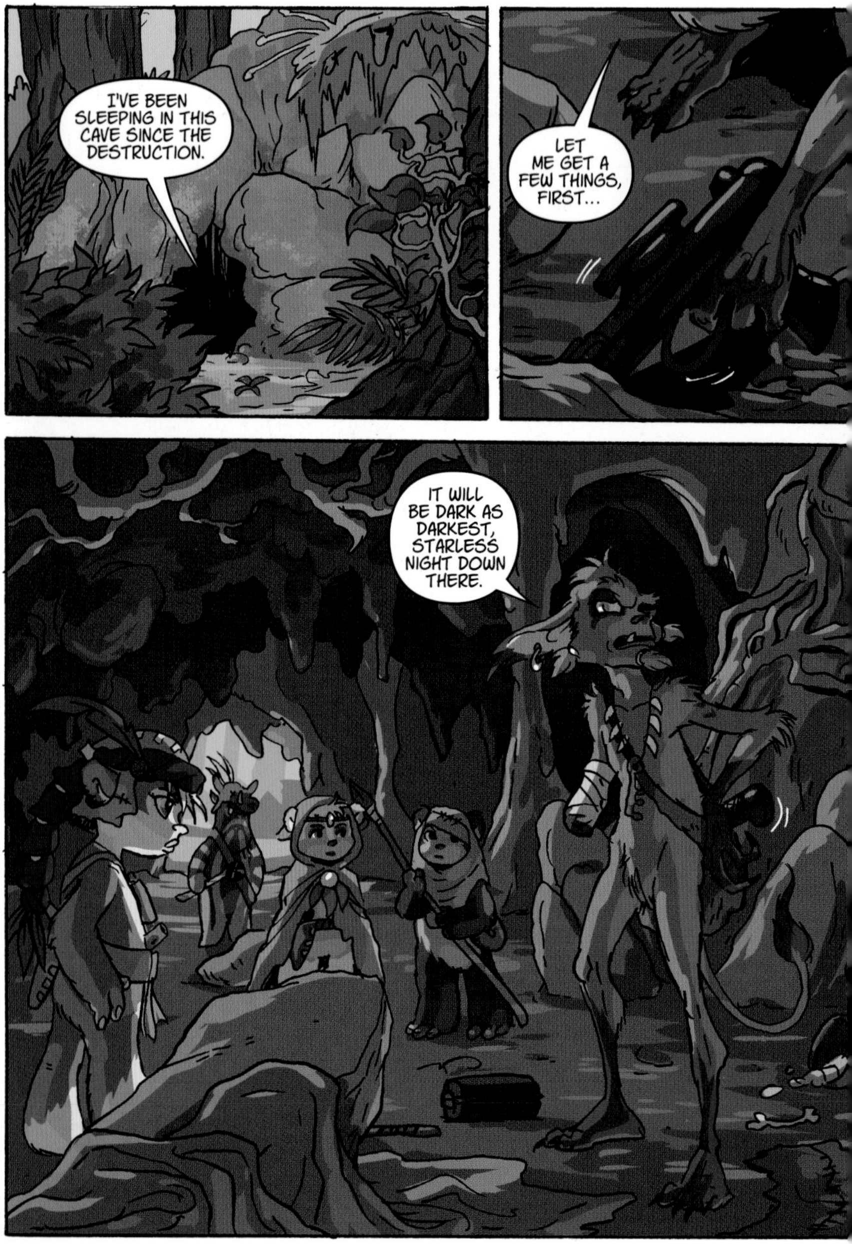
I'VE BEEN SLEEPING IN THIS CAVE SINCE THE DESTRUCTION.
LET ME GET A FEW THINGS, FIRST...
IT WILL BE DARK AS DARKEST, STARLESS NIGHT DOWN THERE.

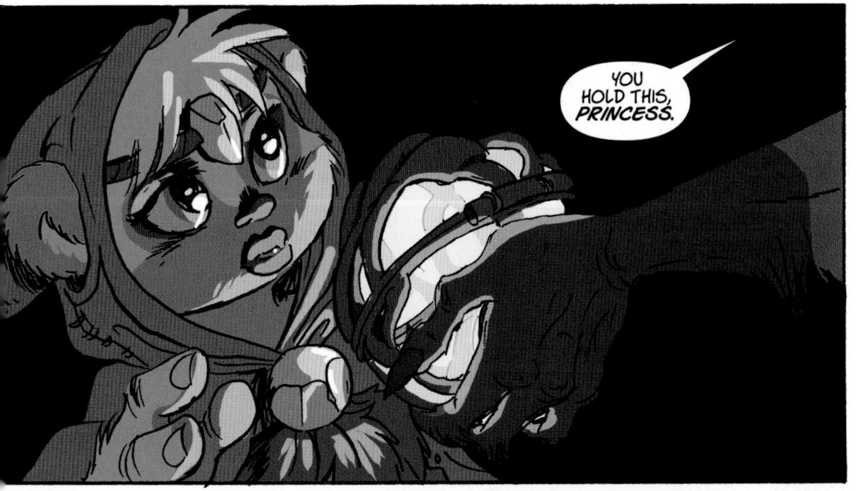
YOU HOLD THIS, *PRINCESS.*

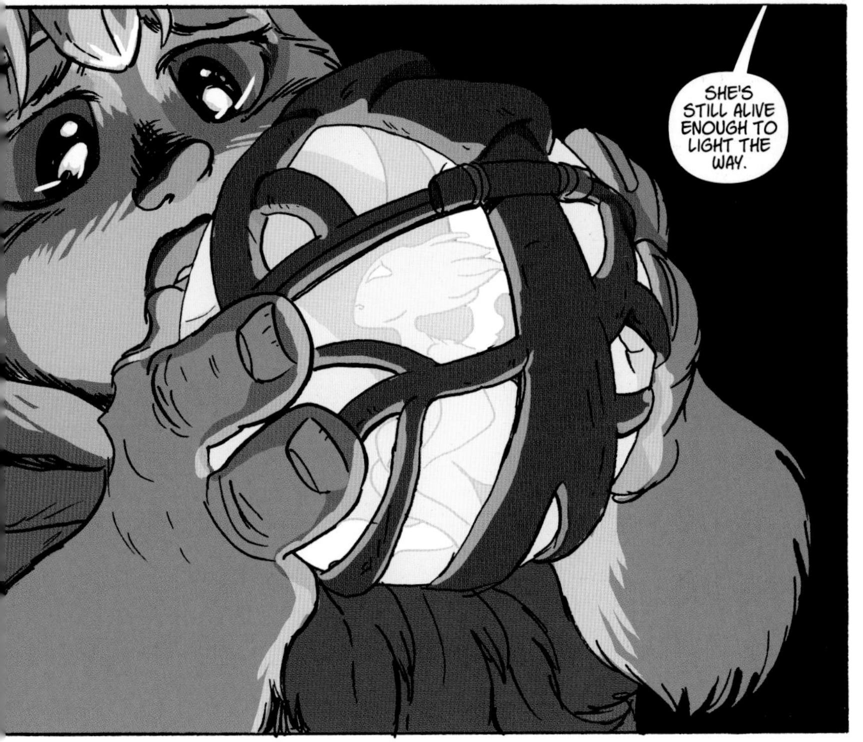
SHE'S STILL ALIVE ENOUGH TO LIGHT THE WAY.

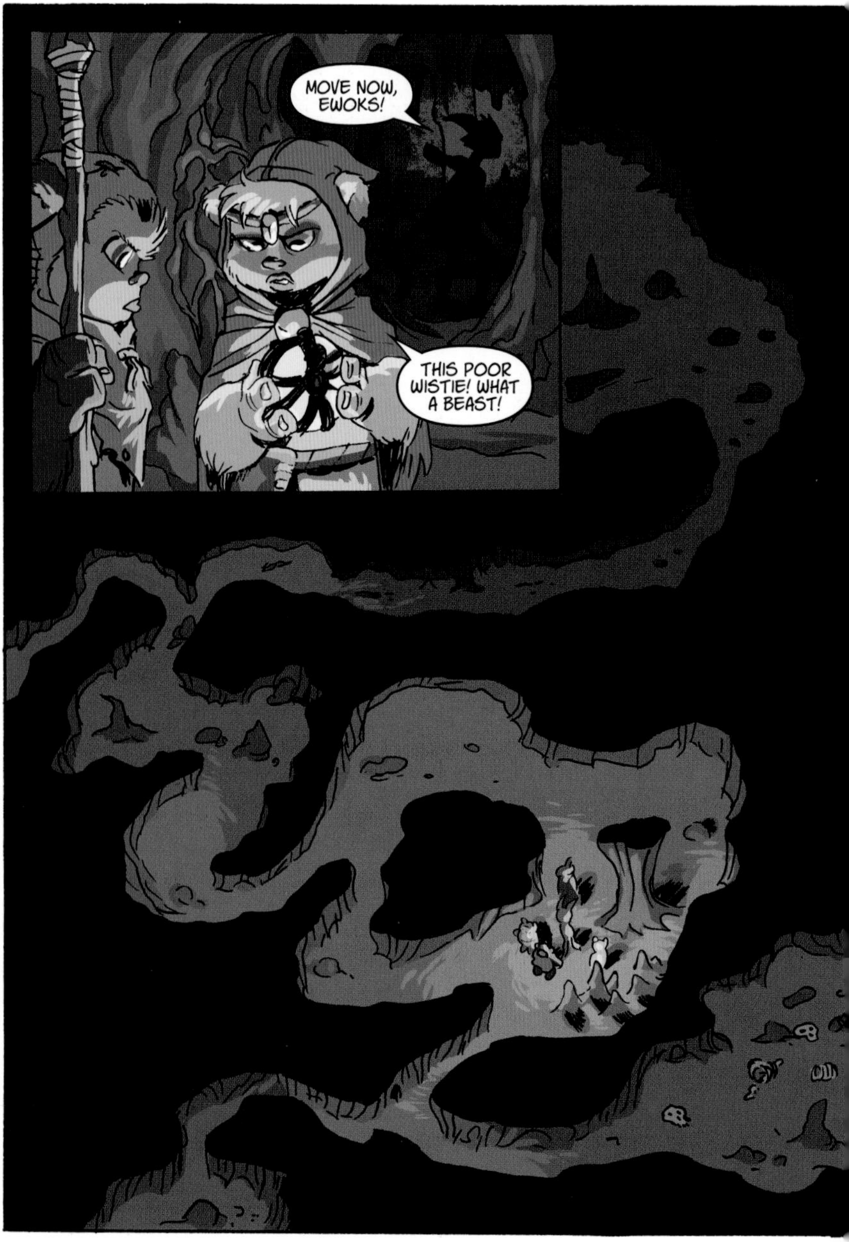
MOVE NOW, EWOKS!
THIS POOR WISTIE! WHAT A BEAST!

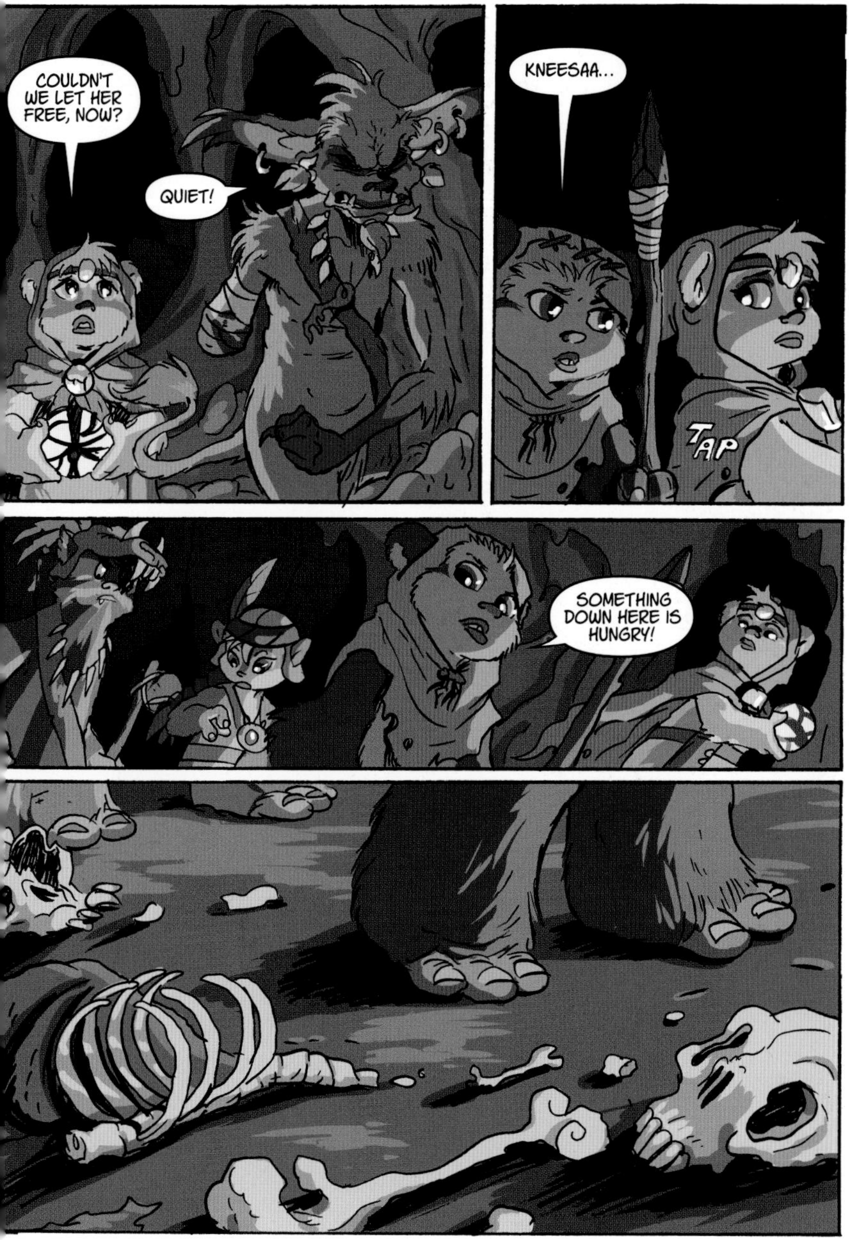
COULDN'T WE LET HER FREE, NOW?
QUIET!
KNEESAA...
TAP
SOMETHING DOWN HERE IS HUNGRY!

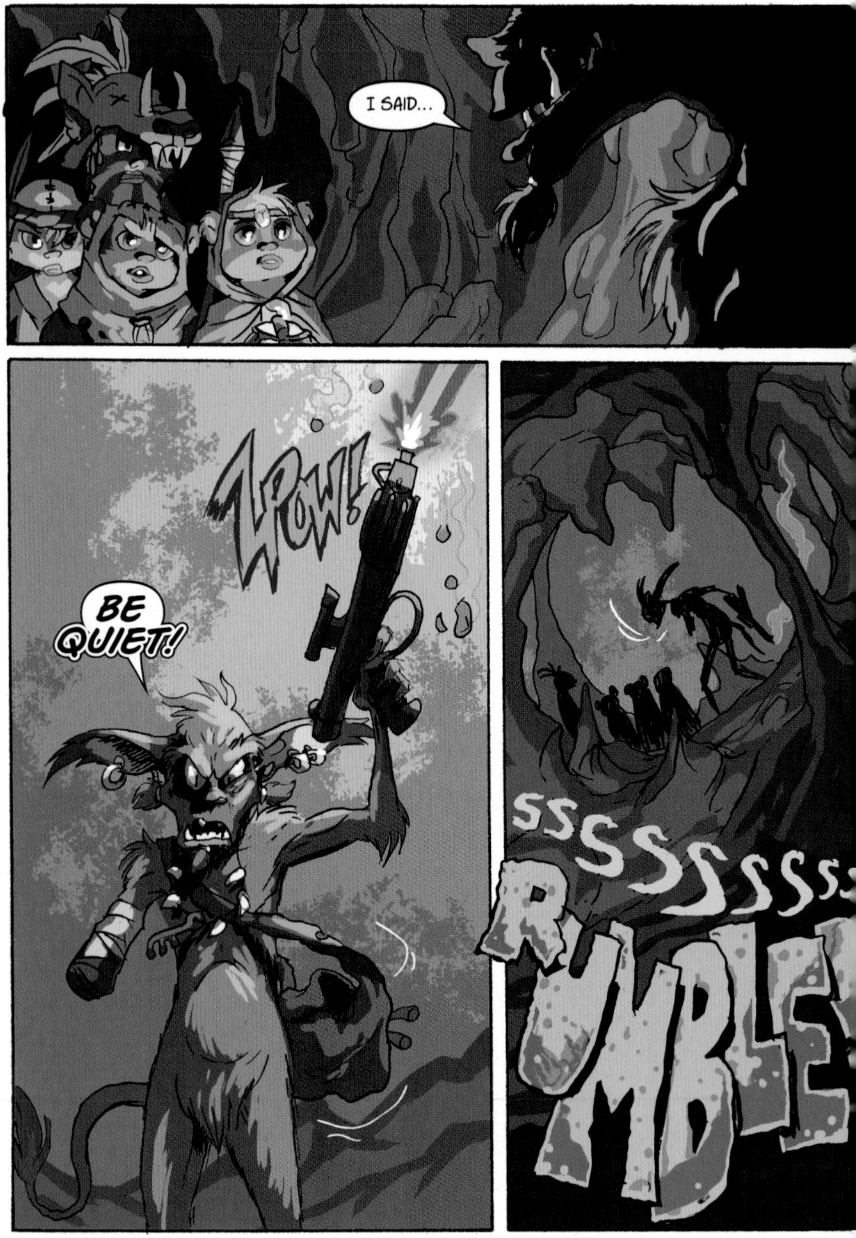
I SAID...
ZPOW!
BE QUIET!
SSSSSSSS
RUMBLE

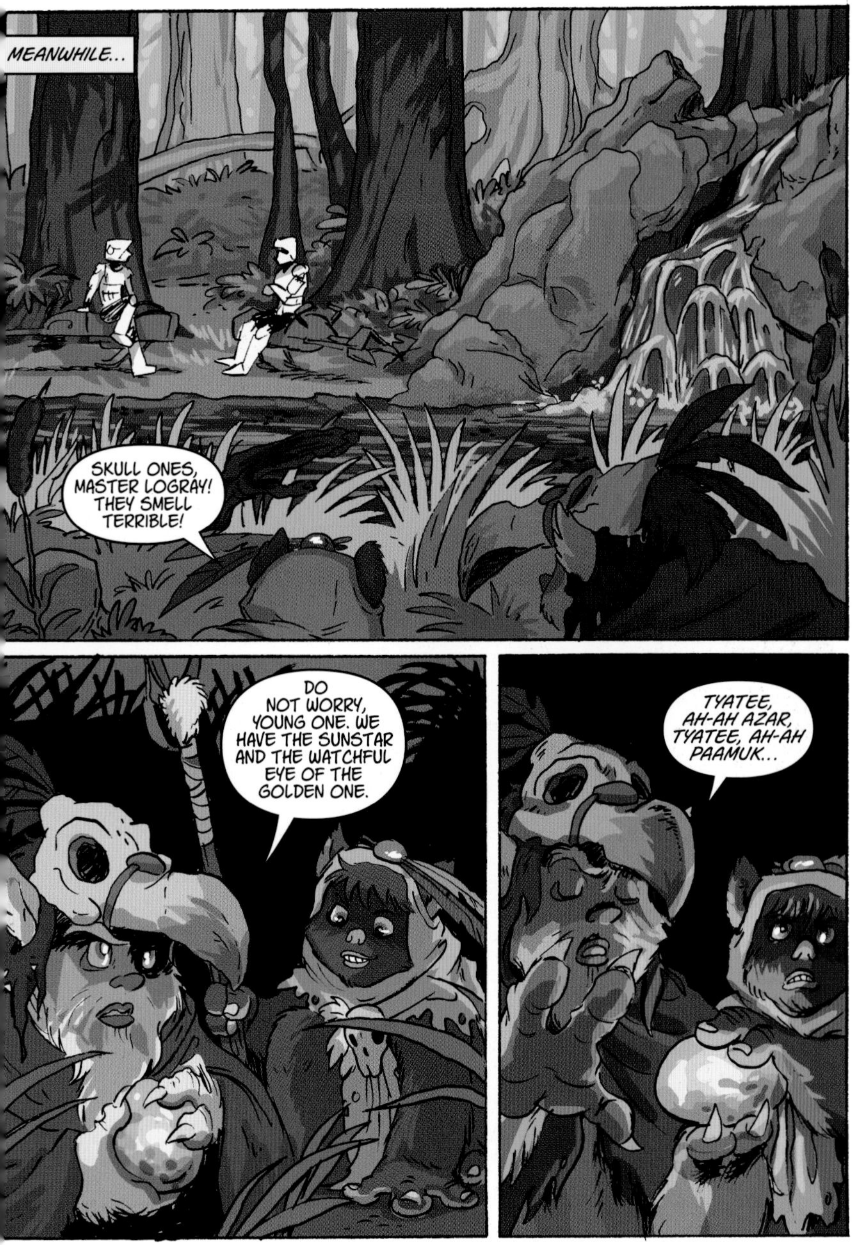
MEANWHILE...
SKULL ONES, MASTER LOGRAY! THEY SMELL TERRIBLE!
DO NOT WORRY, YOUNG ONE. WE HAVE THE SUNSTAR AND THE WATCHFUL EYE OF THE GOLDEN ONE.
TYATEE, AH-AH AZAR, TYATEE, AH-AH PAAMUK...

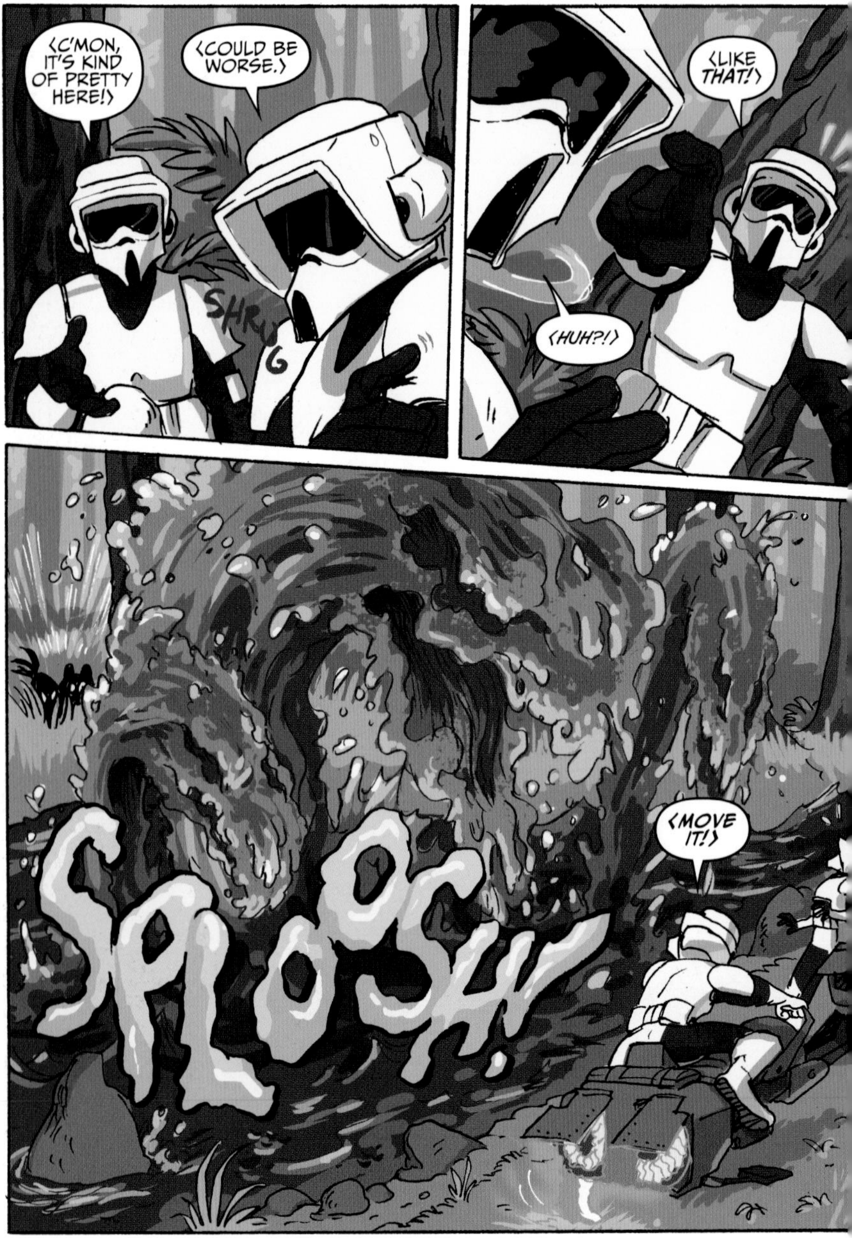

‹C'MON, IT'S KIND OF PRETTY HERE!›
‹COULD BE WORSE.›
SHRUG
‹LIKE THAT!›
‹HUH?!›
SPLOOSH!
‹MOVE IT!›

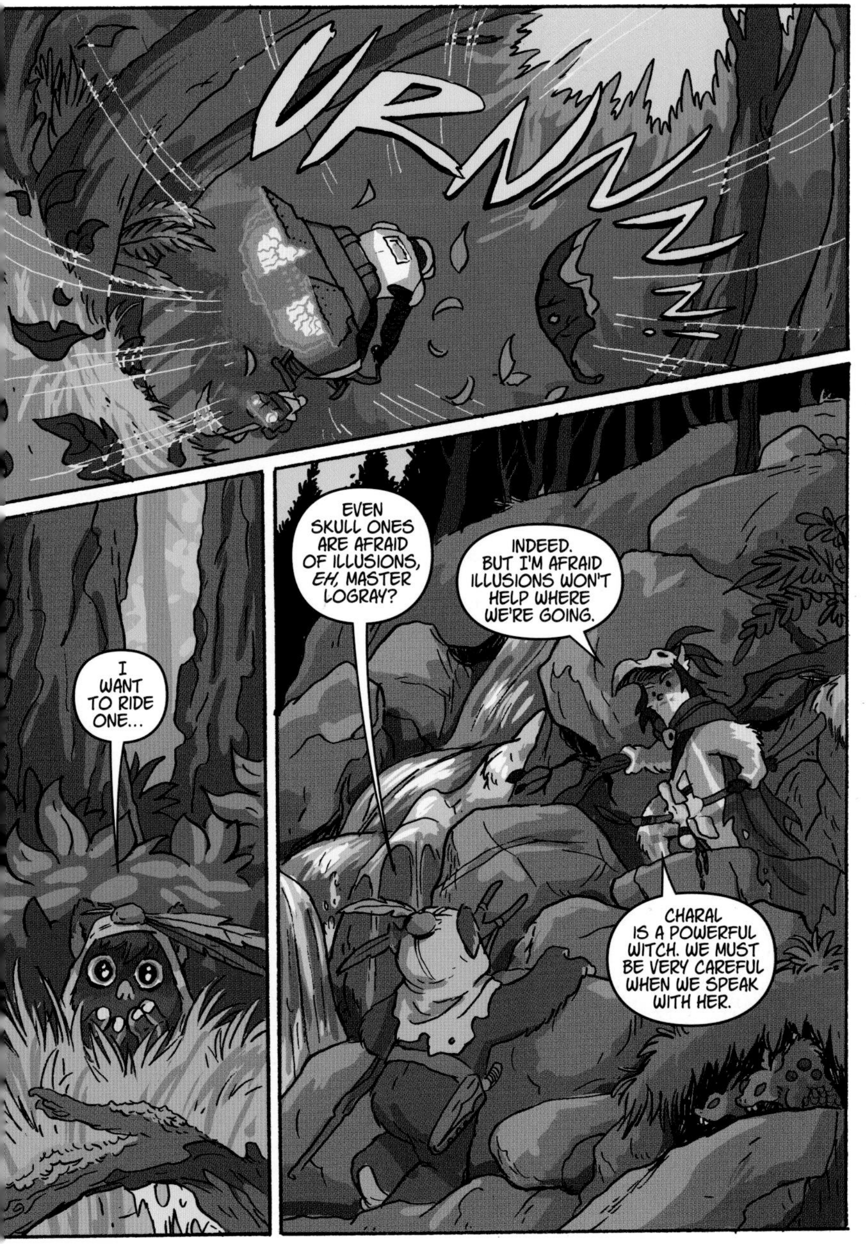
URNNNN!
I WANT TO RIDE ONE...
EVEN SKULL ONES ARE AFRAID OF ILLUSIONS, *EH,* MASTER LOGRAY?
INDEED. BUT I'M AFRAID ILLUSIONS WON'T HELP WHERE WE'RE GOING.
CHARAL IS A POWERFUL WITCH. WE MUST BE VERY CAREFUL WHEN WE SPEAK WITH HER.

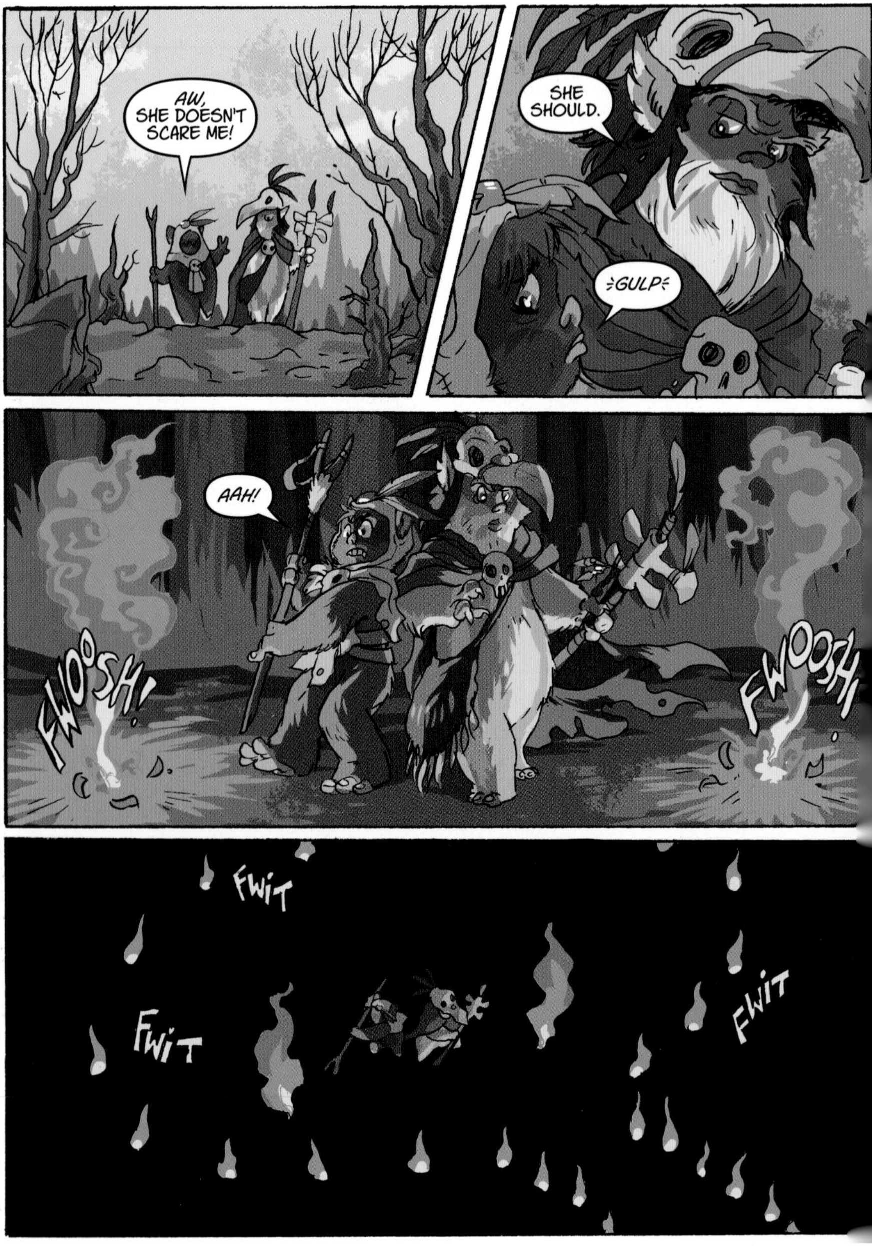
AW, SHE DOESN'T SCARE ME!
SHE SHOULD.
GULP
AAH!
FWOOSH!
FWOOSH!
FWIT
FWIT
FWIT

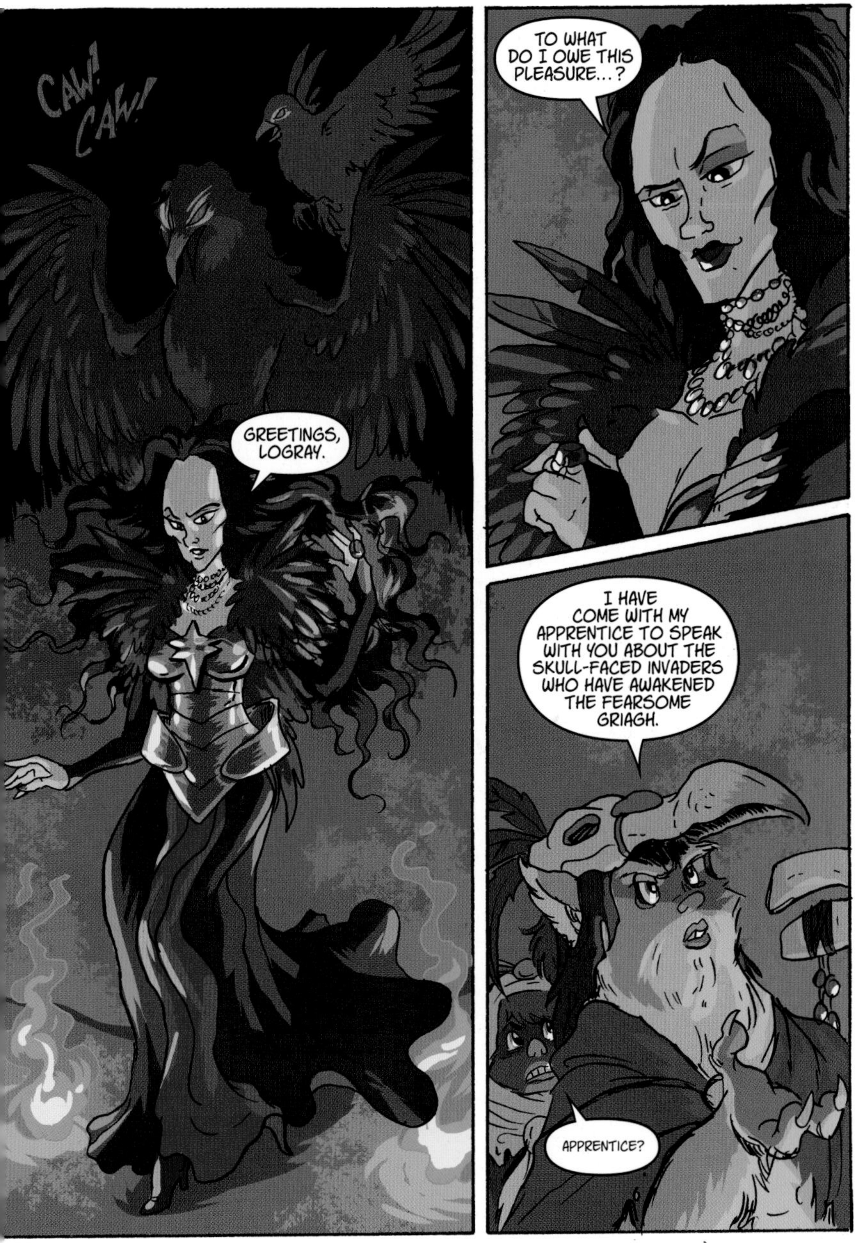
CAW! CAW!
GREETINGS, LOGRAY.
TO WHAT DO I OWE THIS PLEASURE...?
I HAVE COME WITH MY APPRENTICE TO SPEAK WITH YOU ABOUT THE SKULL-FACED INVADERS WHO HAVE AWAKENED THE FEARSOME GRIAGH.
APPRENTICE?

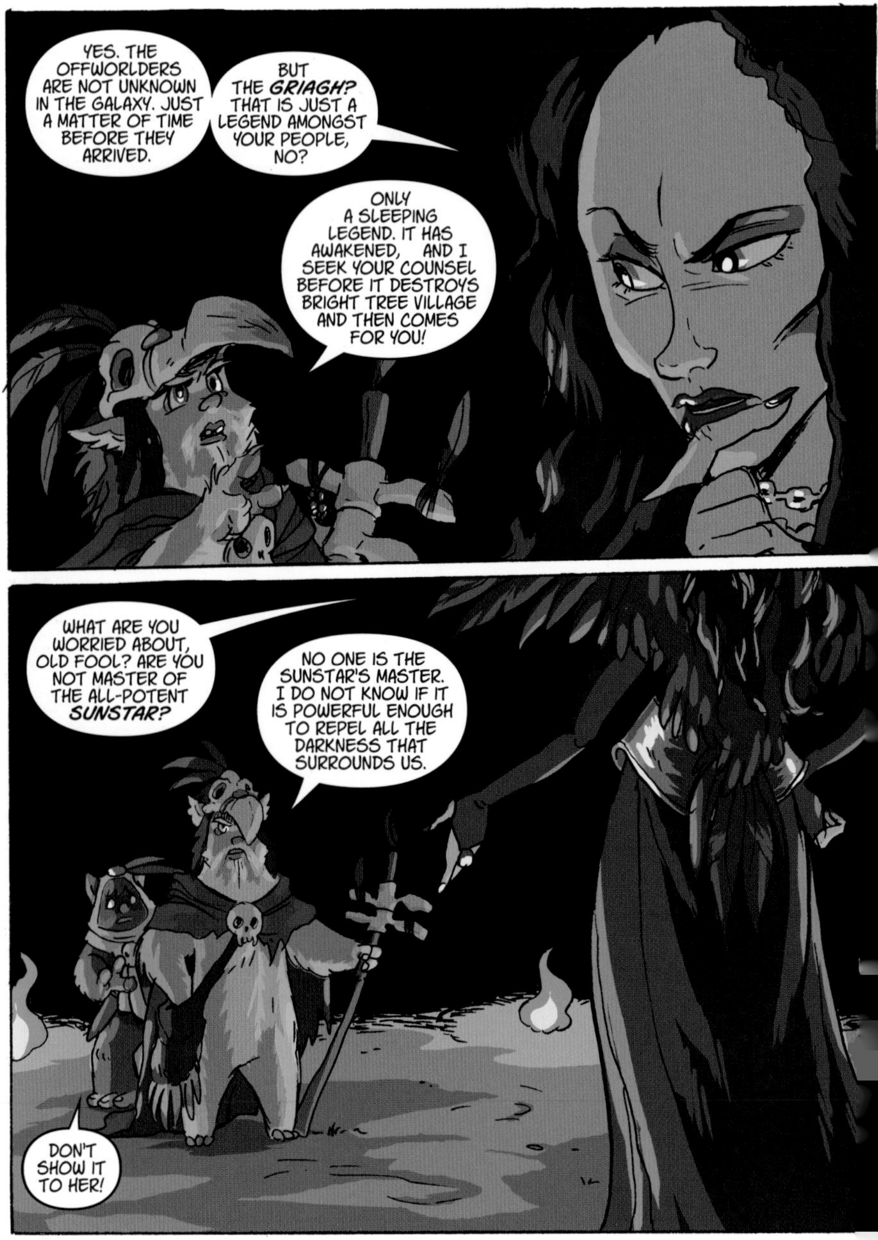
YES. THE OFFWORLDERS ARE NOT UNKNOWN IN THE GALAXY. JUST A MATTER OF TIME BEFORE THEY ARRIVED.
BUT THE *GRIAGH?* THAT IS JUST A LEGEND AMONGST YOUR PEOPLE, NO?
ONLY A SLEEPING LEGEND. IT HAS AWAKENED, AND I SEEK YOUR COUNSEL BEFORE IT DESTROYS BRIGHT TREE VILLAGE AND THEN COMES FOR YOU!
WHAT ARE YOU WORRIED ABOUT, OLD FOOL? ARE YOU NOT MASTER OF THE ALL-POTENT *SUNSTAR?*
NO ONE IS THE SUNSTAR'S MASTER. I DO NOT KNOW IF IT IS POWERFUL ENOUGH TO REPEL ALL THE DARKNESS THAT SURROUNDS US.
DON'T SHOW IT TO HER!

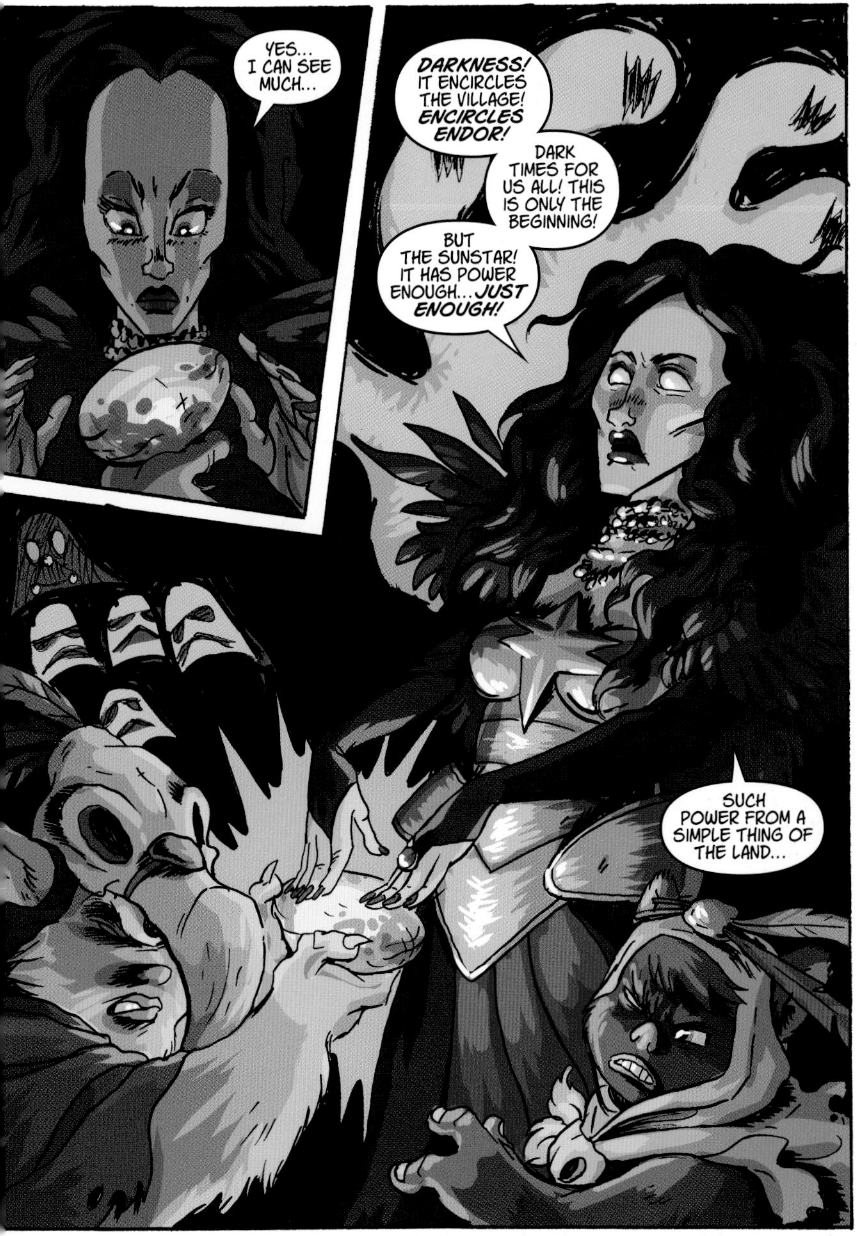
YES... I CAN SEE MUCH...
DARKNESS! IT ENCIRCLES THE VILLAGE! ENCIRCLES ENDOR!
DARK TIMES FOR US ALL! THIS IS ONLY THE BEGINNING!
BUT THE SUNSTAR! IT HAS POWER ENOUGH... JUST ENOUGH!
SUCH POWER FROM A SIMPLE THING OF THE LAND...

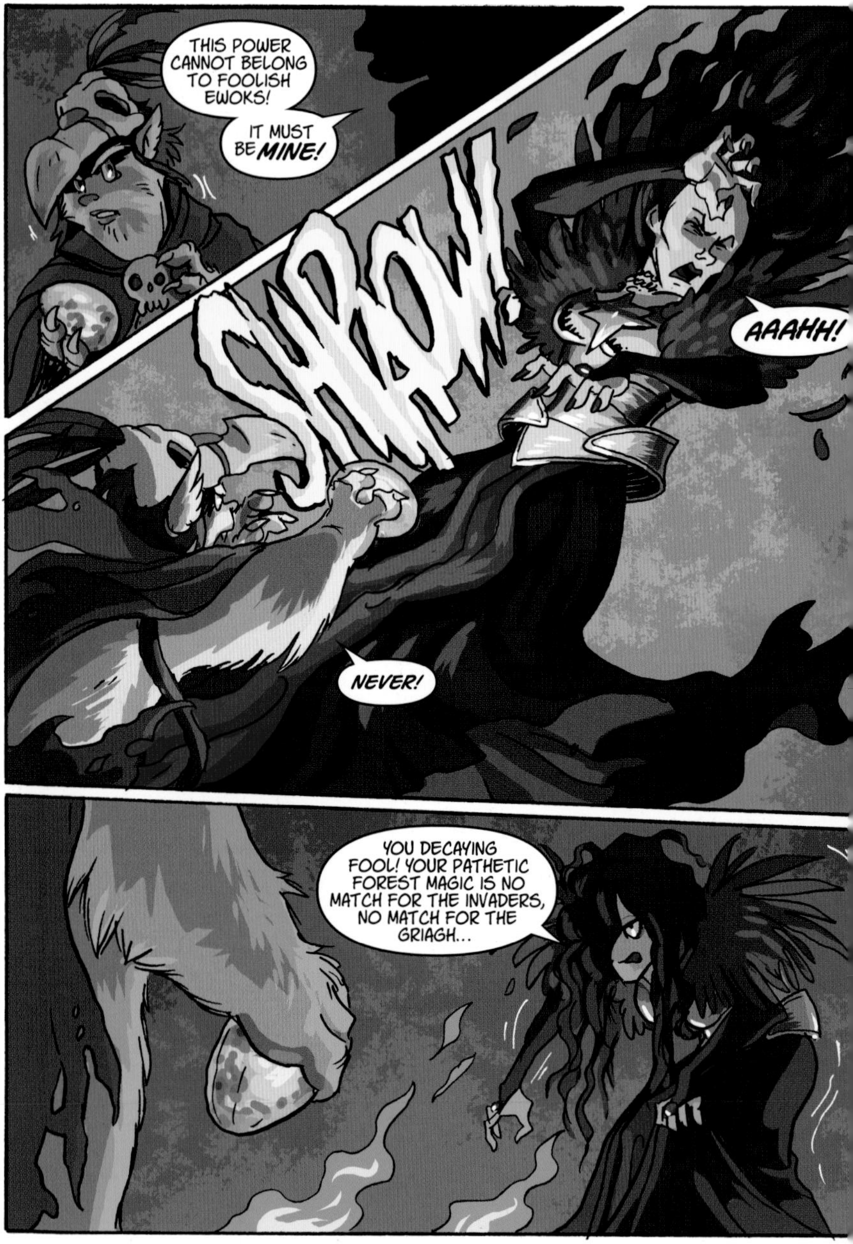
THIS POWER CANNOT BELONG TO FOOLISH EWOKS!
IT MUST BE MINE!
SHRAKK!
AAAHH!
NEVER!
YOU DECAYING FOOL! YOUR PATHETIC FOREST MAGIC IS NO MATCH FOR THE INVADERS, NO MATCH FOR THE GRIAGH...

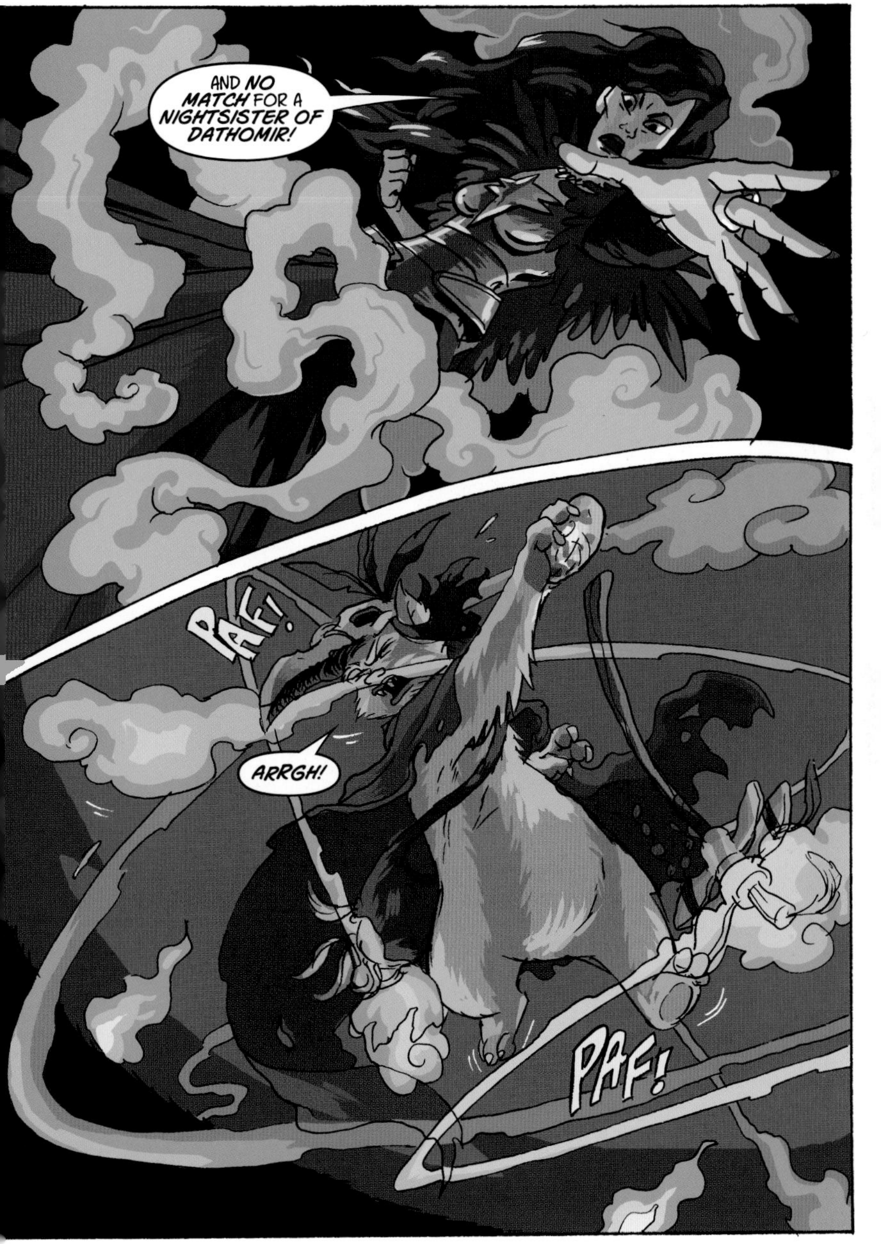
AND NO MATCH FOR A NIGHTSISTER OF DATHOMIR!
PAF!
ARRGH!
PAF!

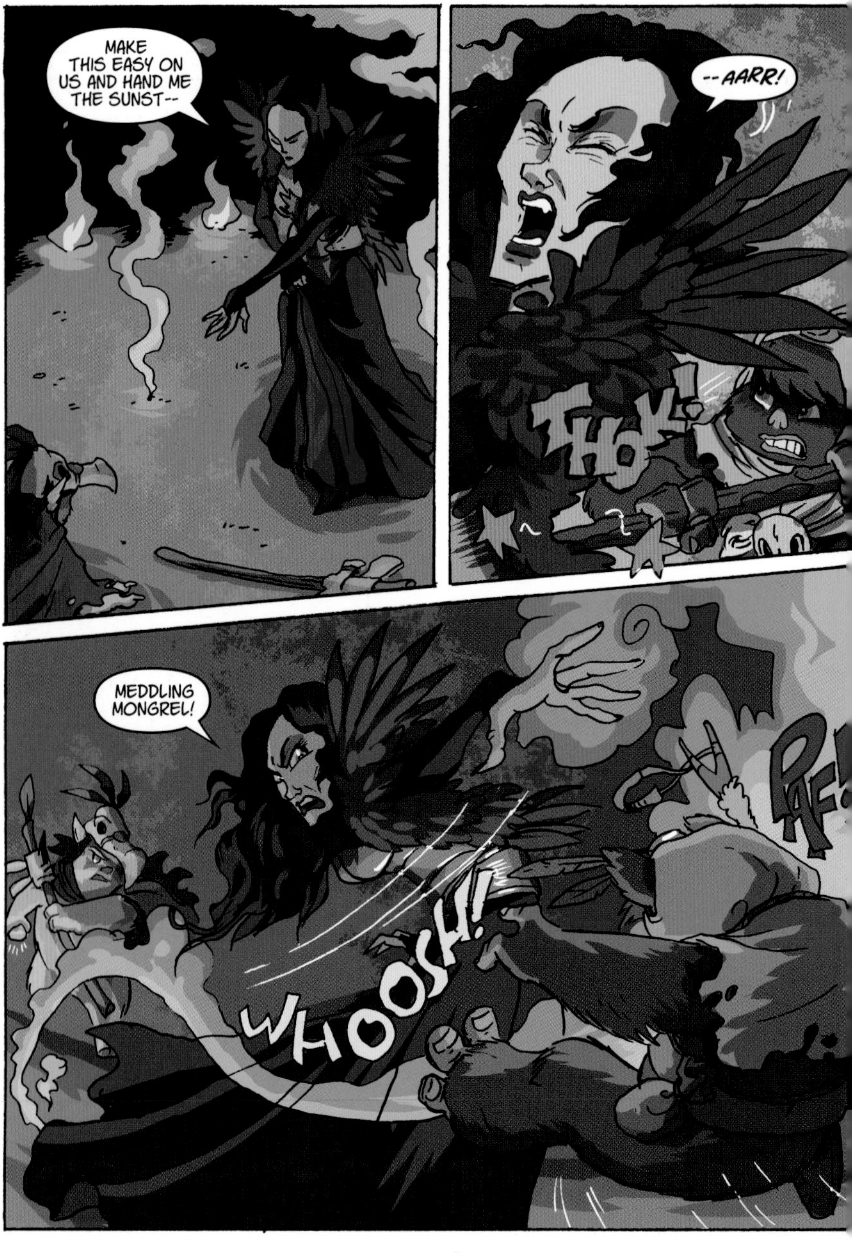
MAKE THIS EASY ON US AND HAND ME THE SUNST--
--AARR!
THOK!
MEDDLING MONGREL!
PAF!
WHOOSH!

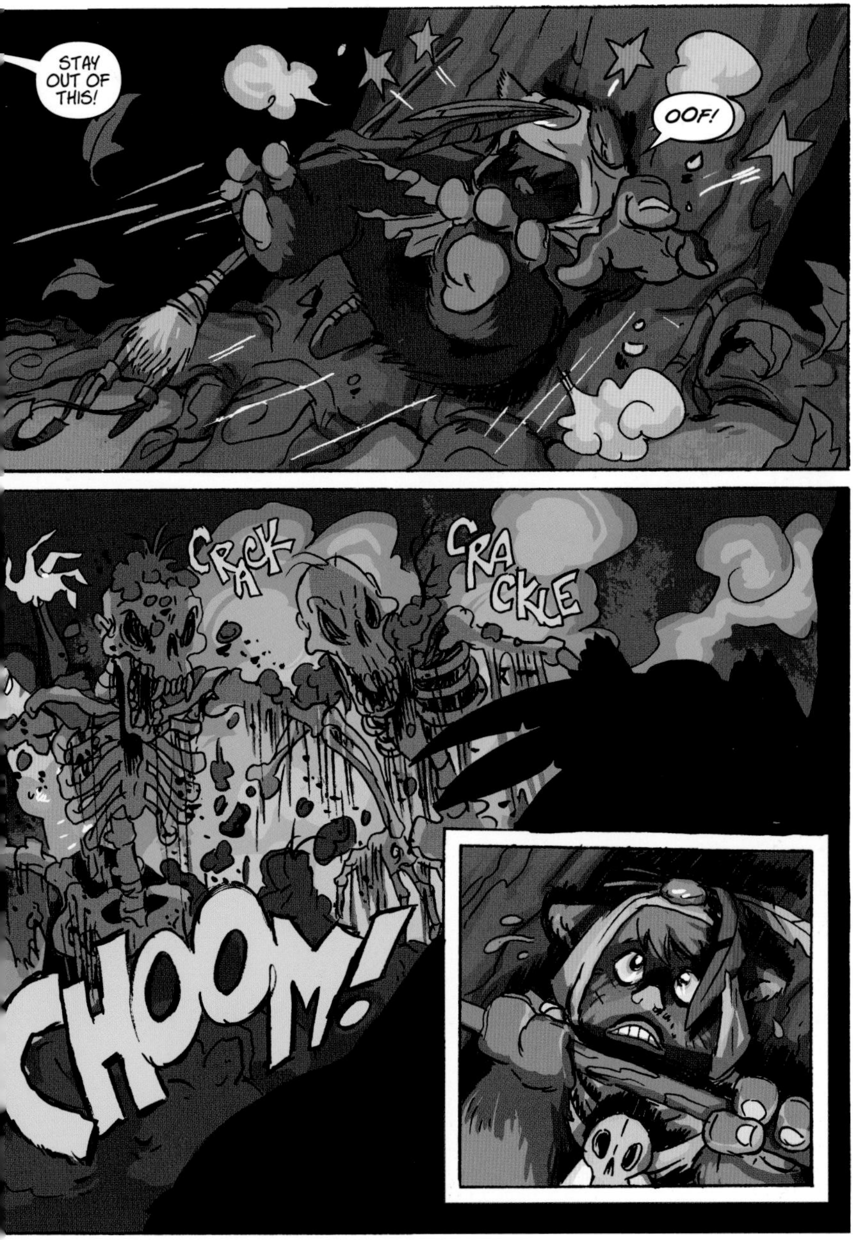
STAY OUT OF THIS!
OOF!
CRACK
CRACKLE
CHOOM!

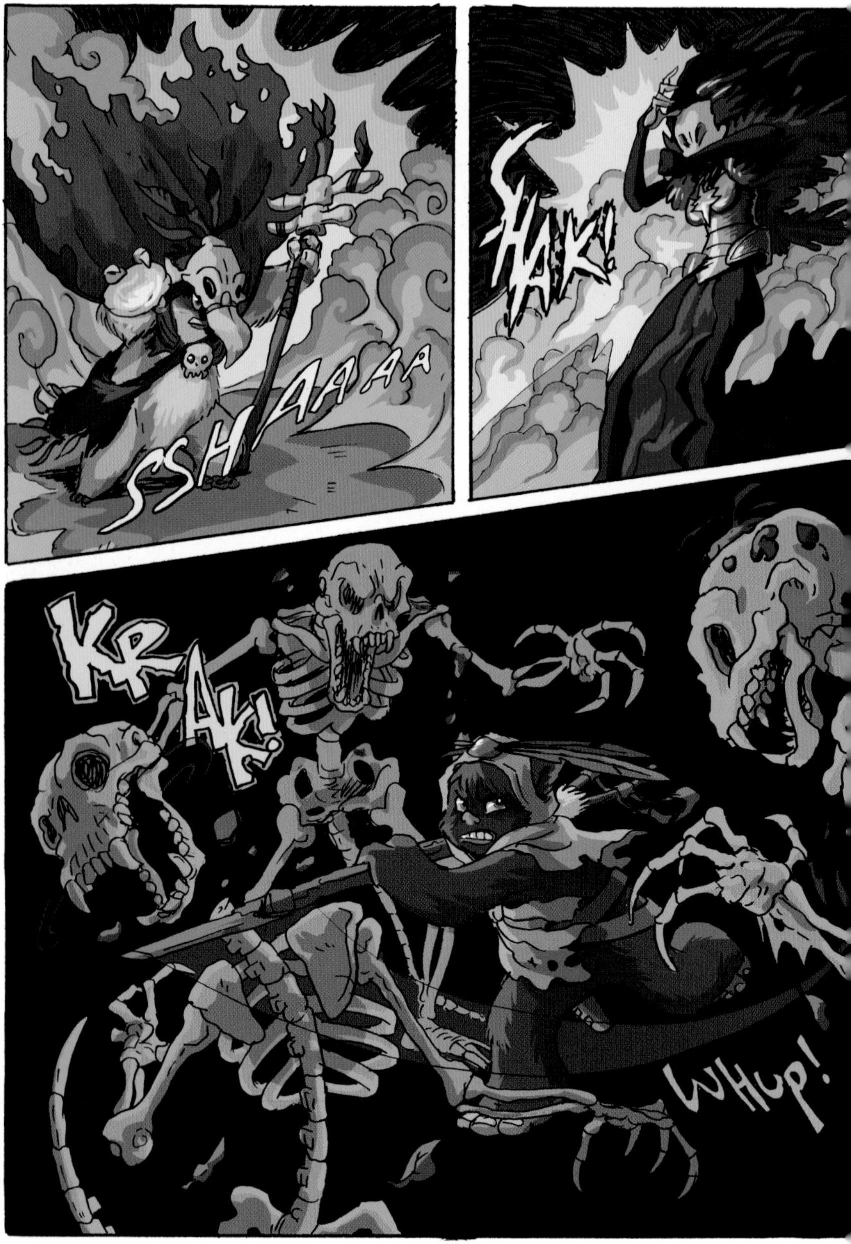
SSHAAAAA
HAK!
KRAK!
WHUP!

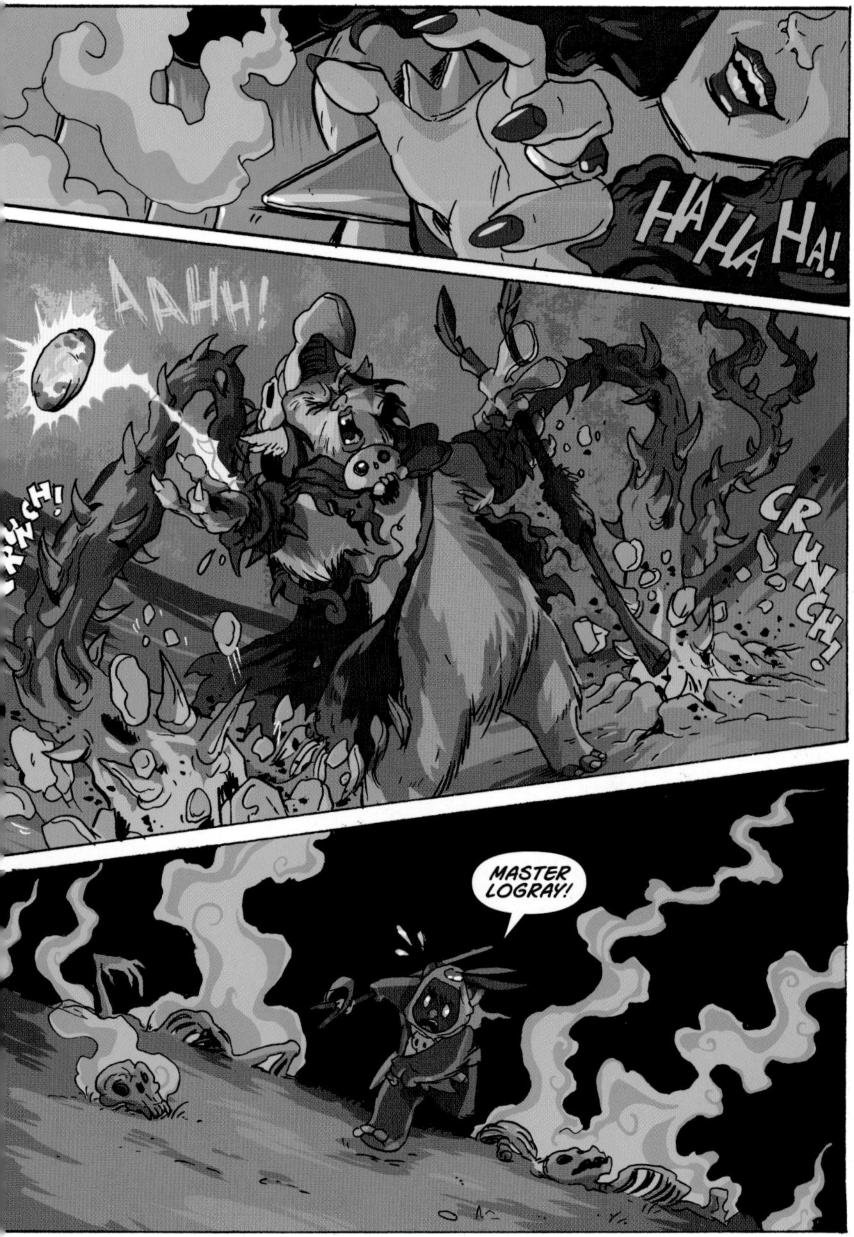
HA HA HA HA!
AAHH!
CRUNCH!
MASTER LOGRAY!

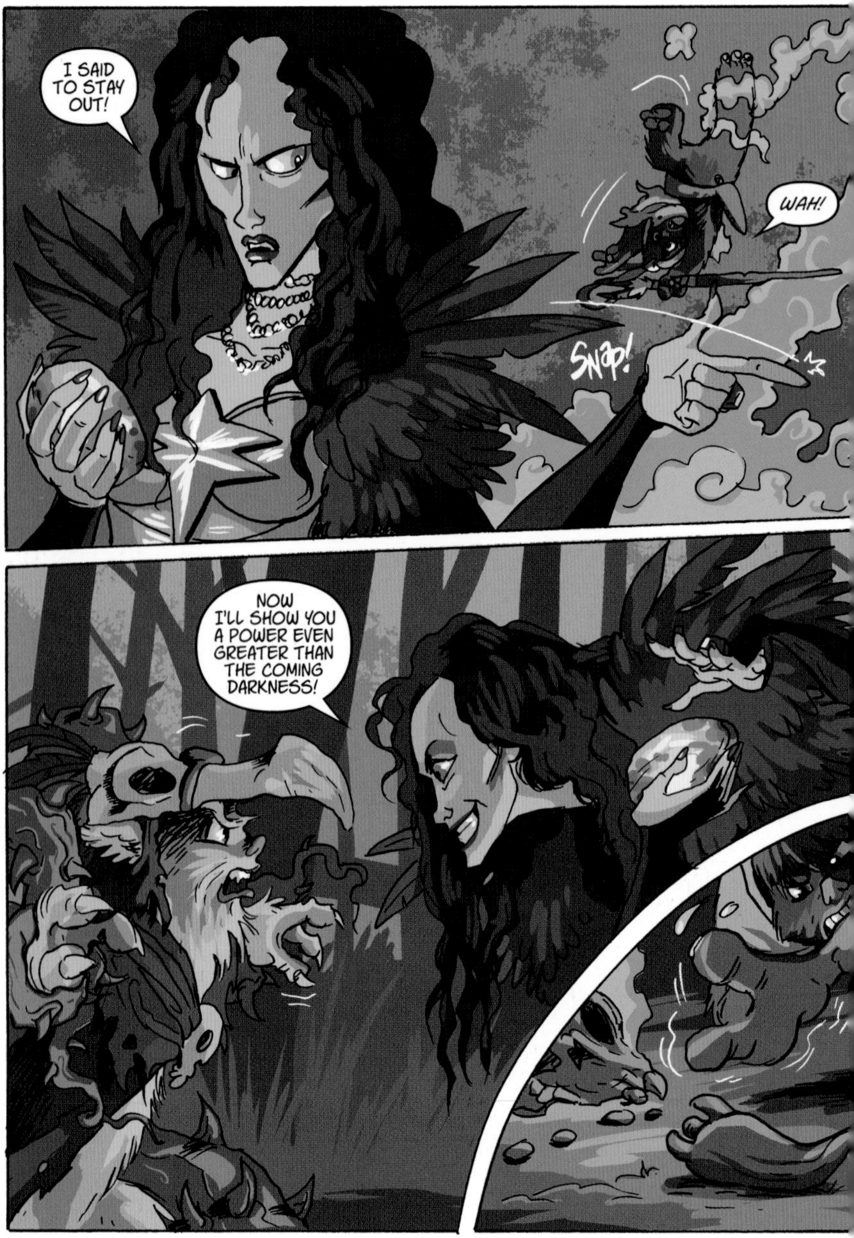
I SAID TO STAY OUT!
WAH!
SNAP!
NOW I'LL SHOW YOU A POWER EVEN GREATER THAN THE COMING DARKNESS!

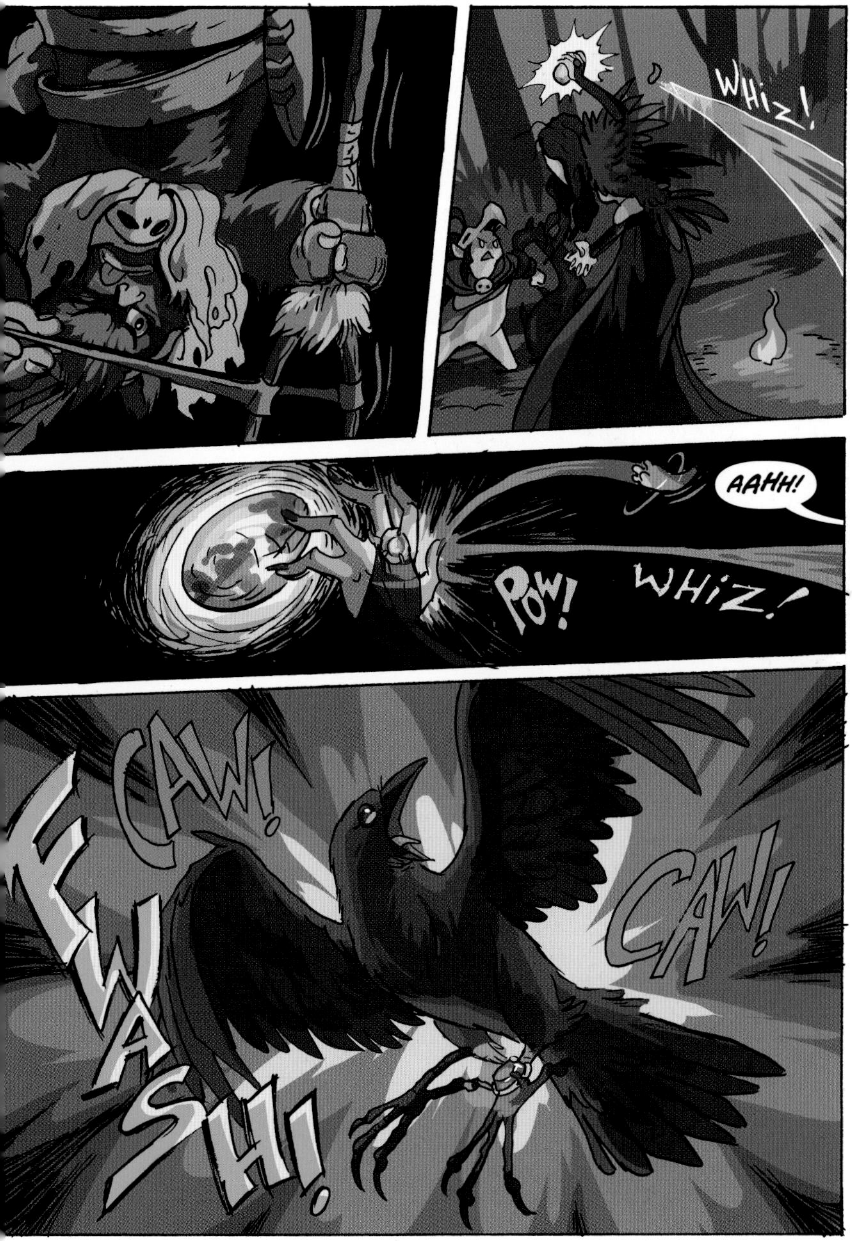
WHIZ!
AAHH!
POW!
WHIZ!
CAW!
FWASH!
CAW!

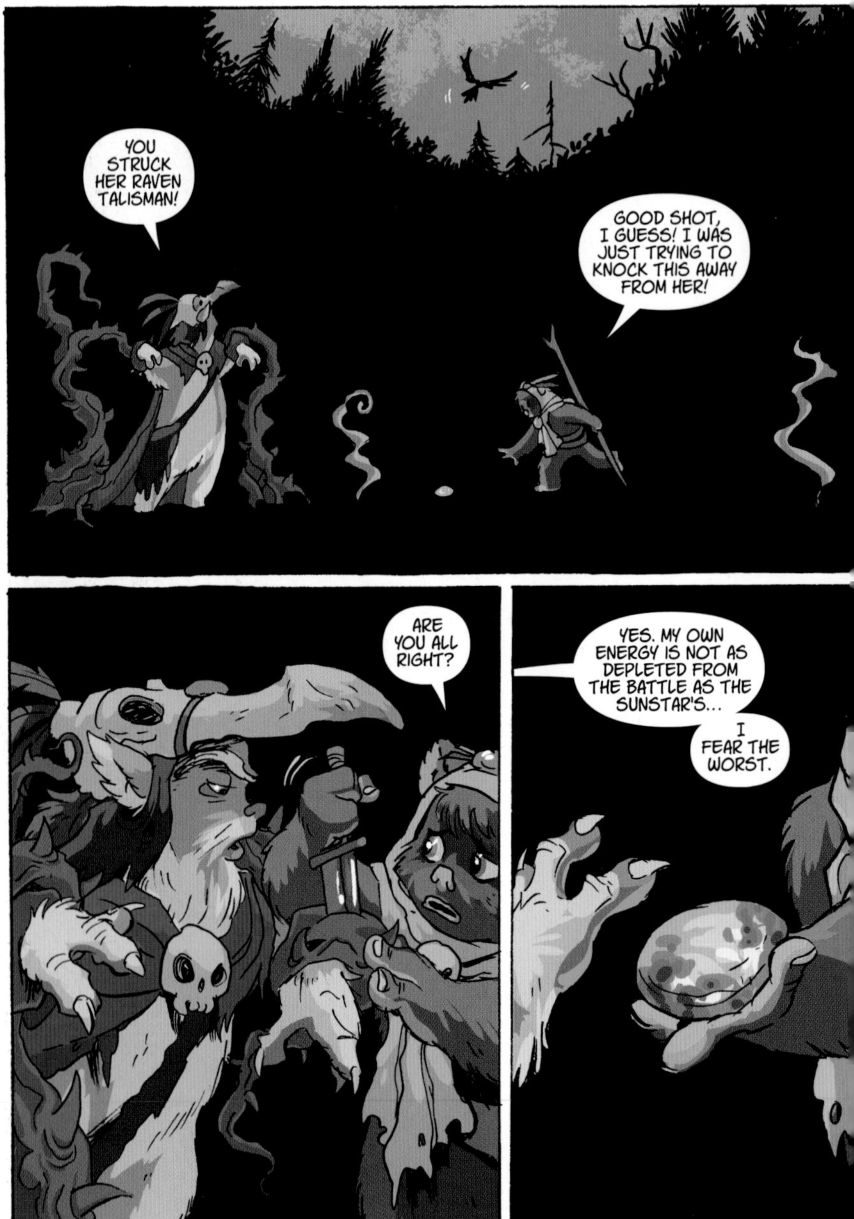
YOU STRUCK HER RAVEN TALISMAN!
GOOD SHOT, I GUESS! I WAS JUST TRYING TO KNOCK THIS AWAY FROM HER!
ARE YOU ALL RIGHT?
YES. MY OWN ENERGY IS NOT AS DEPLETED FROM THE BATTLE AS THE SUNSTAR'S...
I FEAR THE WORST.

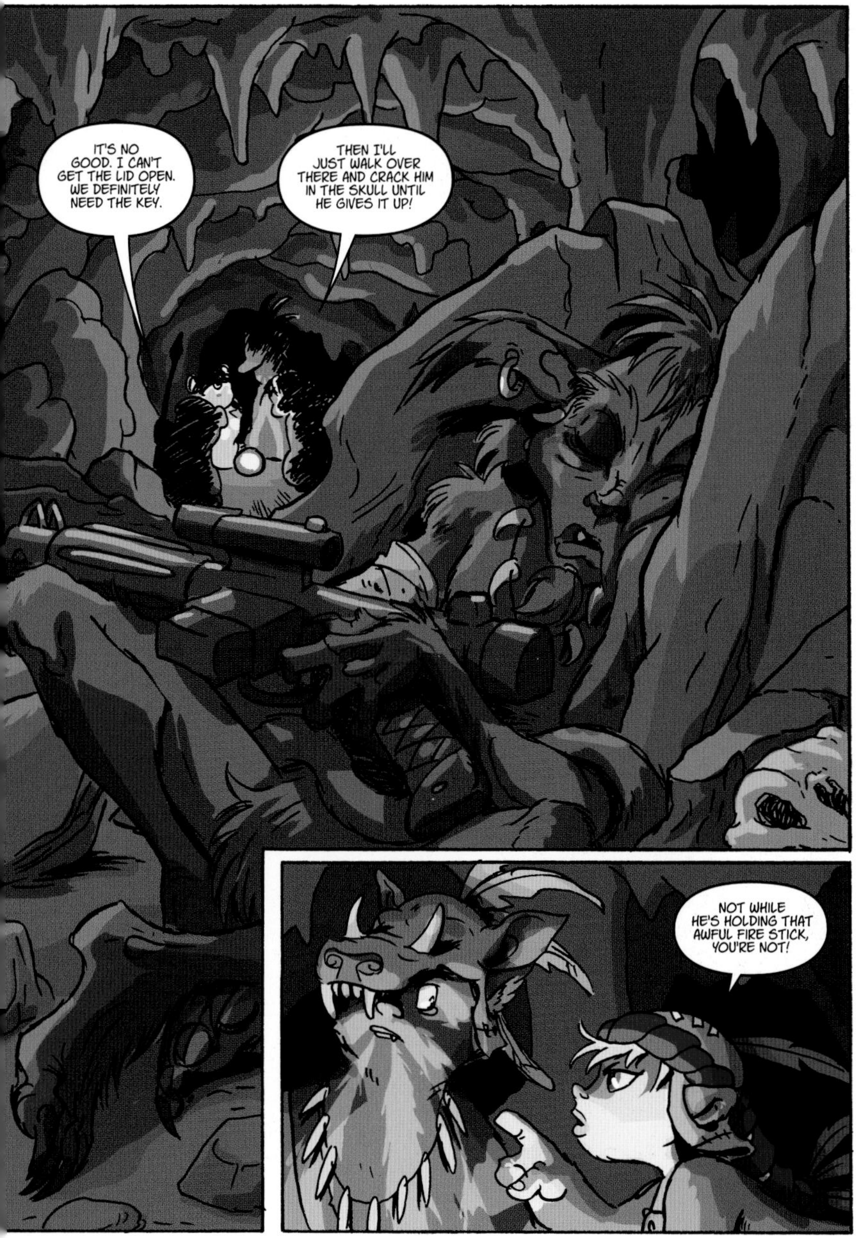
IT'S NO GOOD. I CAN'T GET THE LID OPEN. WE DEFINITELY NEED THE KEY.
THEN I'LL JUST WALK OVER THERE AND CRACK HIM IN THE SKULL UNTIL HE GIVES IT UP!
NOT WHILE HE'S HOLDING THAT AWFUL FIRE STICK, YOU'RE NOT!

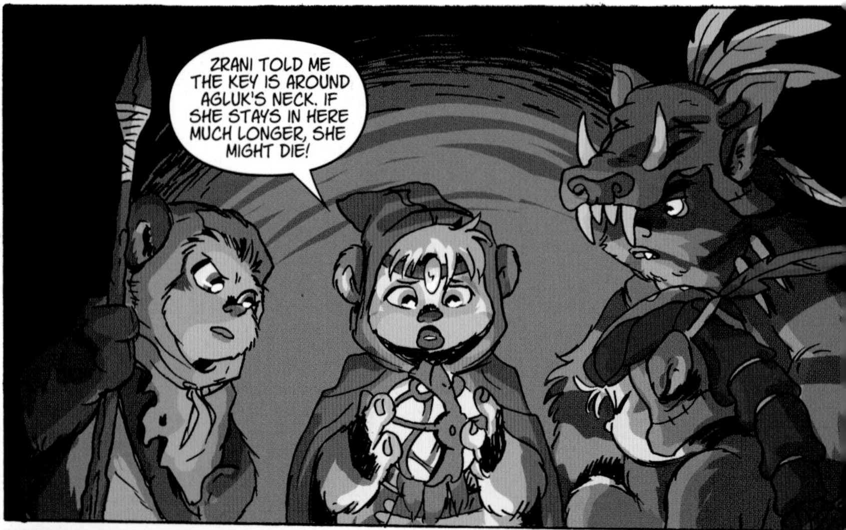
ZRANI TOLD ME THE KEY IS AROUND AGLUK'S NECK. IF SHE STAYS IN HERE MUCH LONGER, SHE MIGHT DIE!

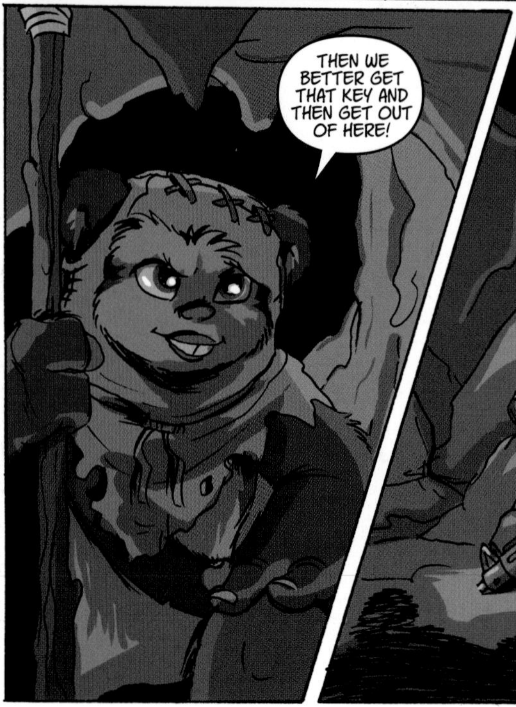
THEN WE BETTER GET THAT KEY AND THEN GET OUT OF HERE!

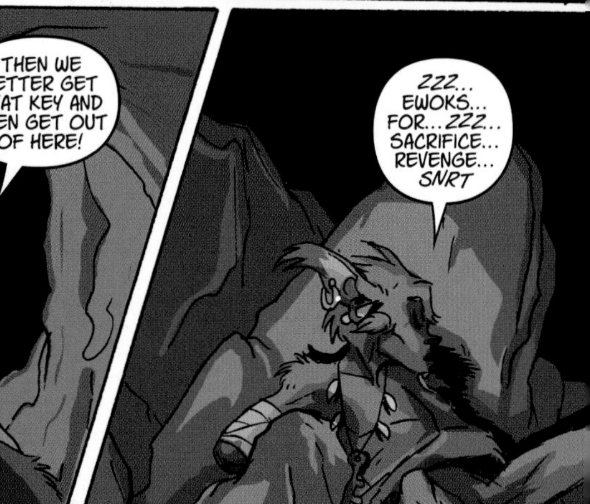
ZZZ... EWOKS... FOR... *ZZZ*... SACRIFICE... REVENGE... *SNRT*

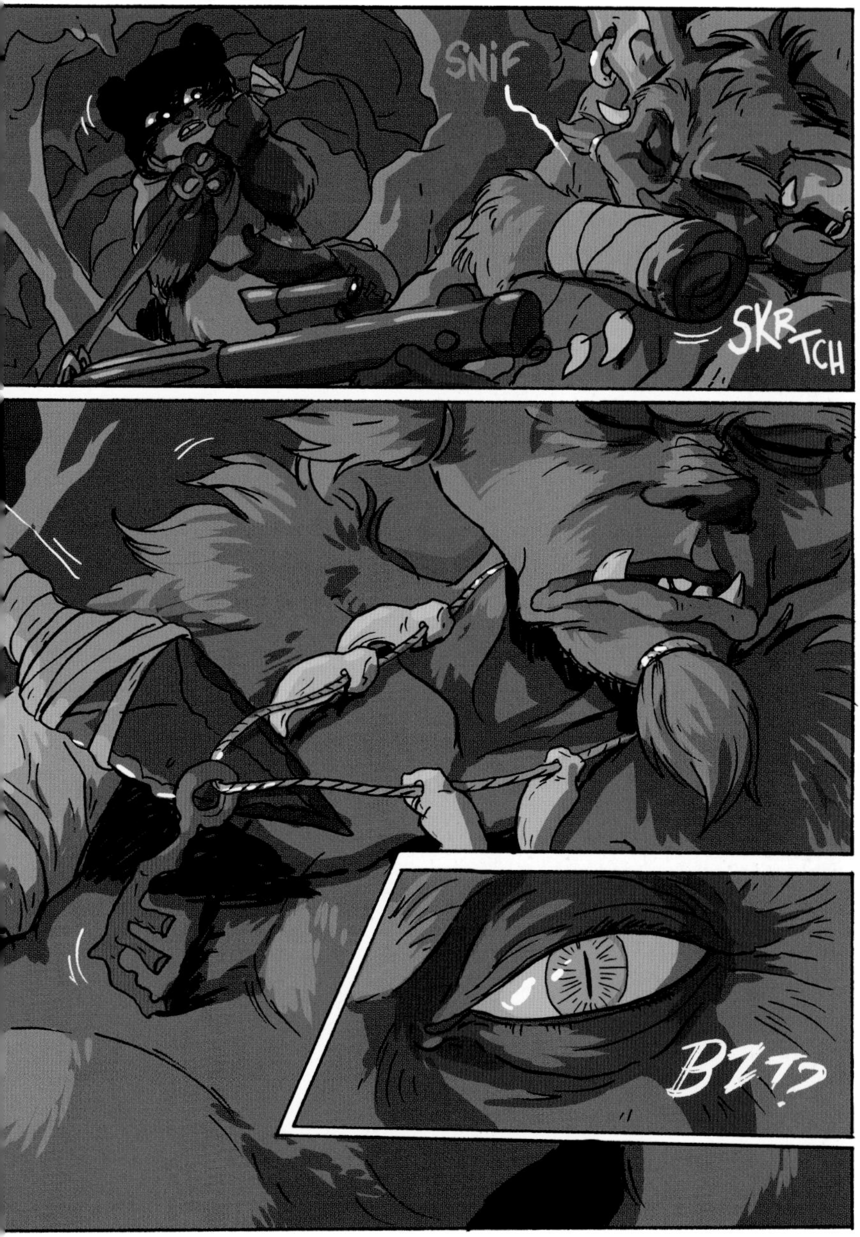
SNIF
SKRTCH
BZT?

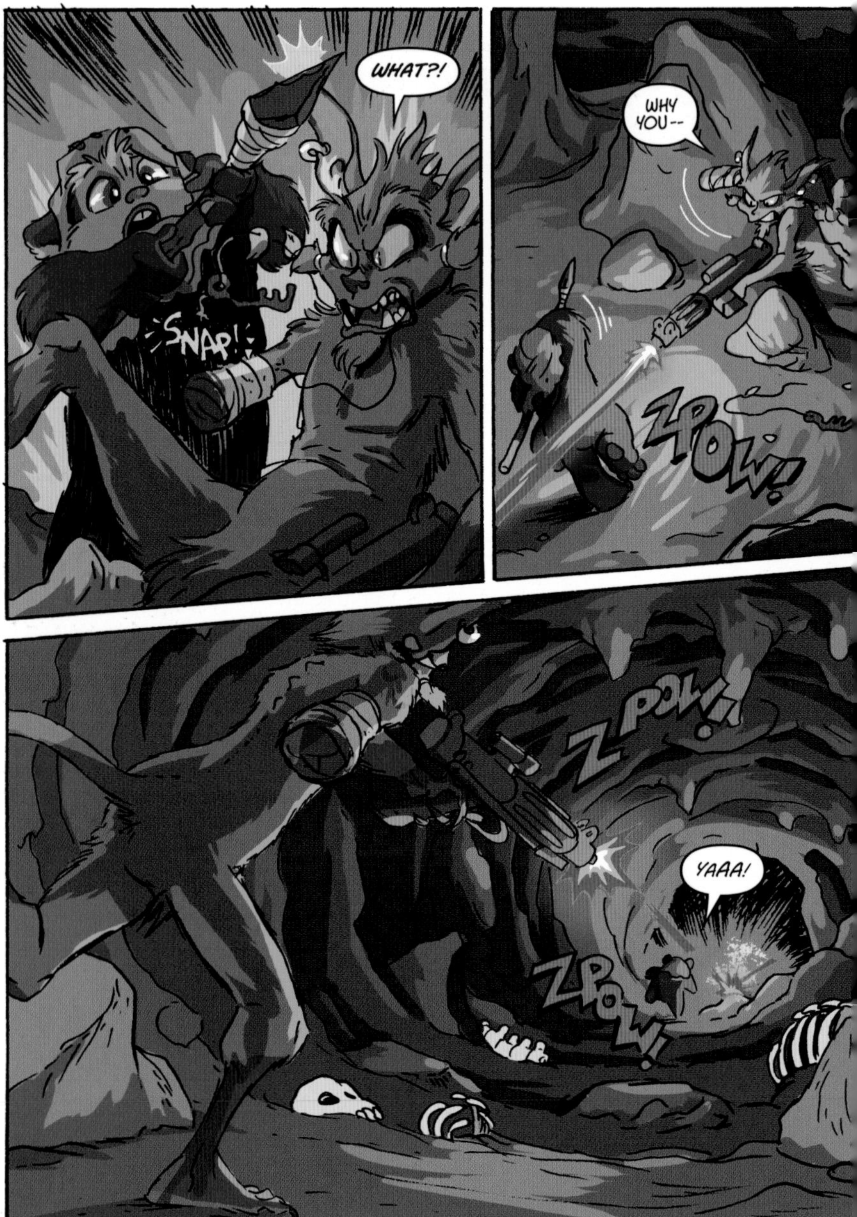
WHAT?!
SNAP!
WHY YOU--
ZPOW!
ZPOW!
YAAA!
ZPOW!

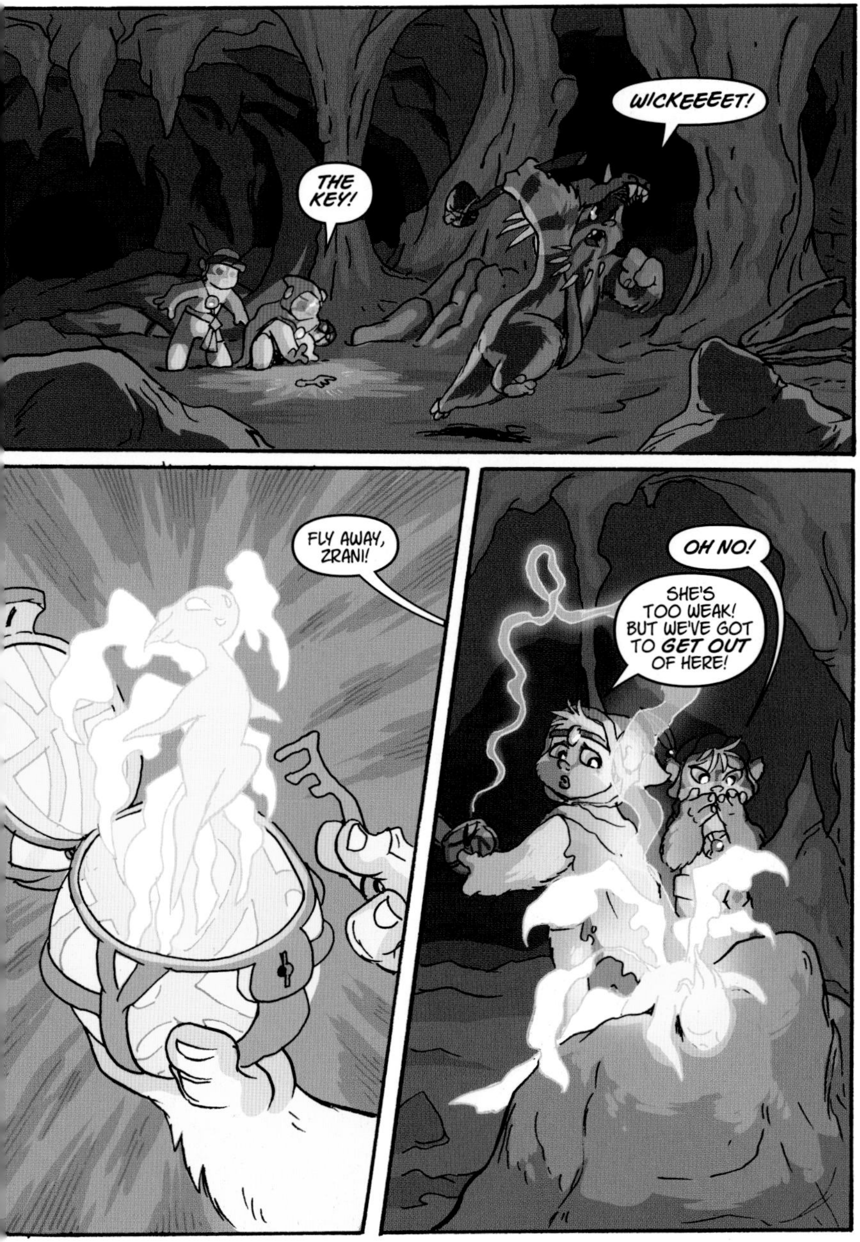
WICKEEEET!
THE KEY!
FLY AWAY, ZRANI!
OH NO!
SHE'S TOO WEAK! BUT WE'VE GOT TO **GET OUT** OF HERE!

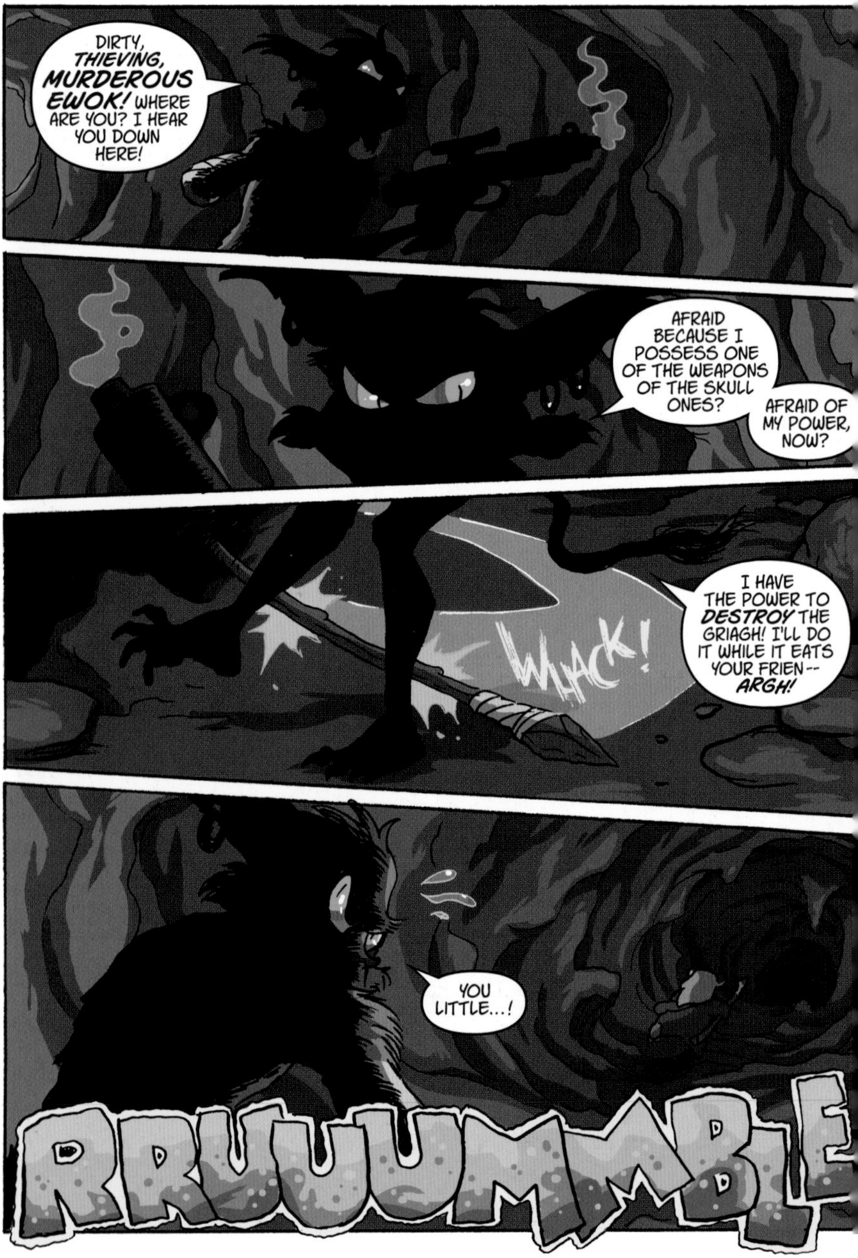
DIRTY, THIEVING, MURDEROUS EWOK! WHERE ARE YOU? I HEAR YOU DOWN HERE!
AFRAID BECAUSE I POSSESS ONE OF THE WEAPONS OF THE SKULL ONES?
AFRAID OF MY POWER, NOW?
WHACK!
I HAVE THE POWER TO DESTROY THE GRIAGH! I'LL DO IT WHILE IT EATS YOUR FRIEN-- ARGH!
YOU LITTLE...!
RRUUUMMBLE

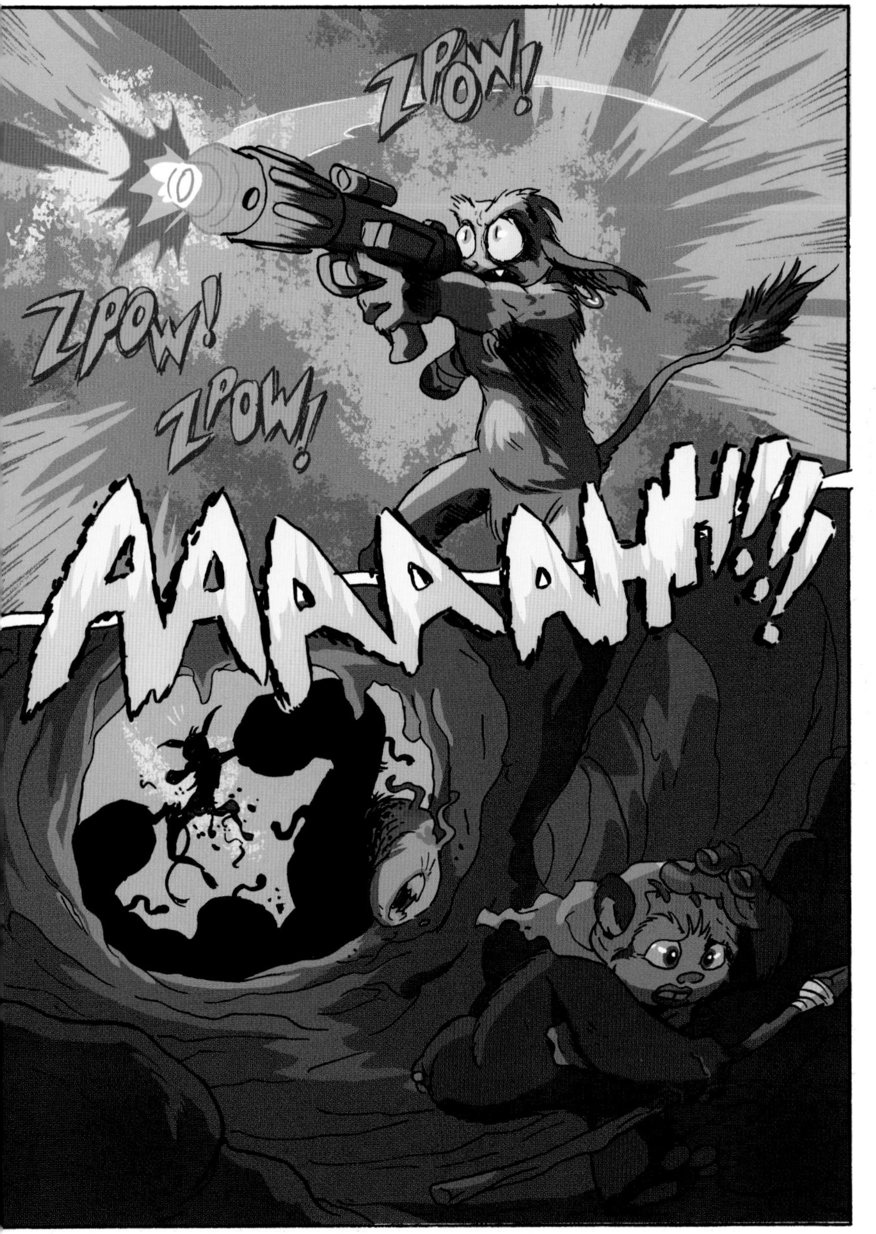
ZPOW!
ZPOW!
ZPOW!
AAAAAH!!!

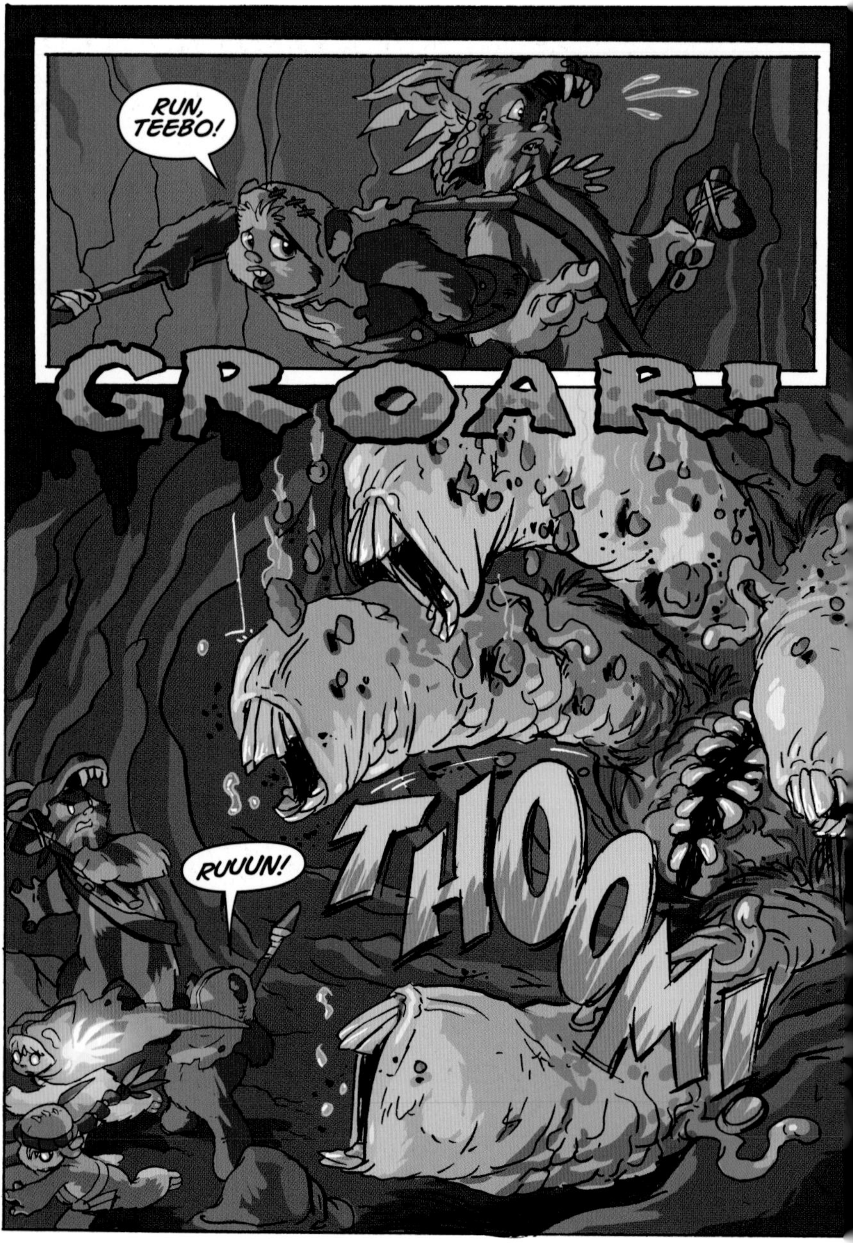
RUN, TEEBO!
GROAR!
RUUUN!
THOOM!

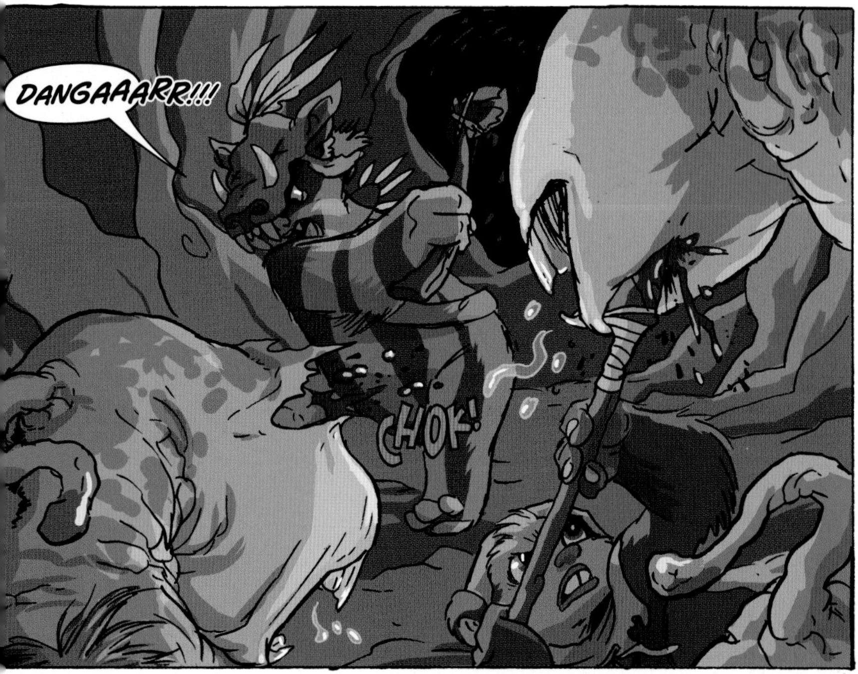
DANGAAARR!!!
CHOK!

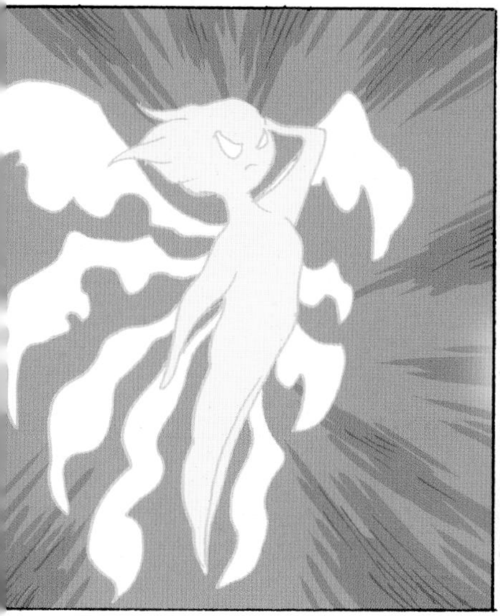

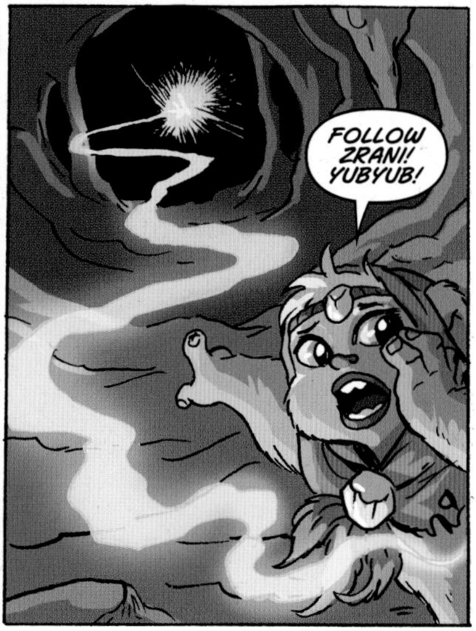
FOLLOW ZRANI! YUBYUB!

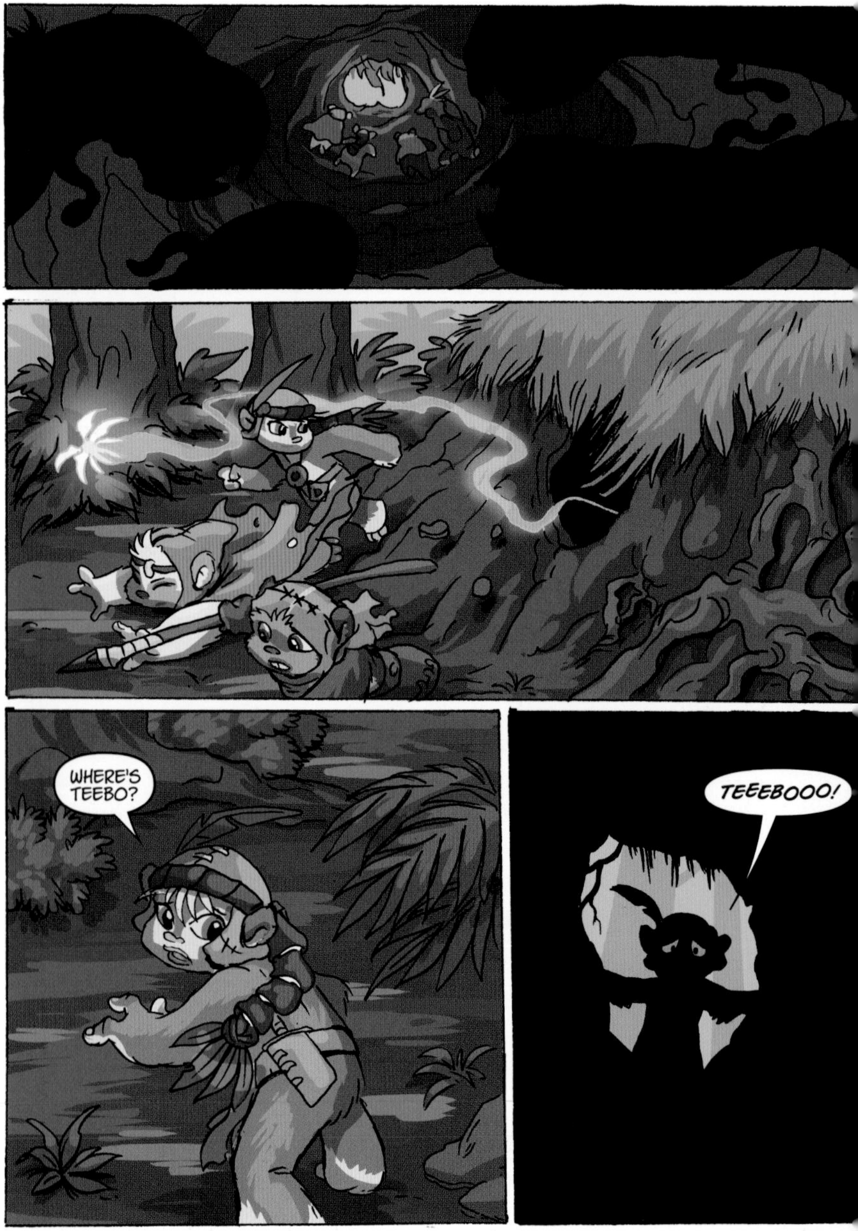
WHERE'S TEEBO?
TEEEBOOO!

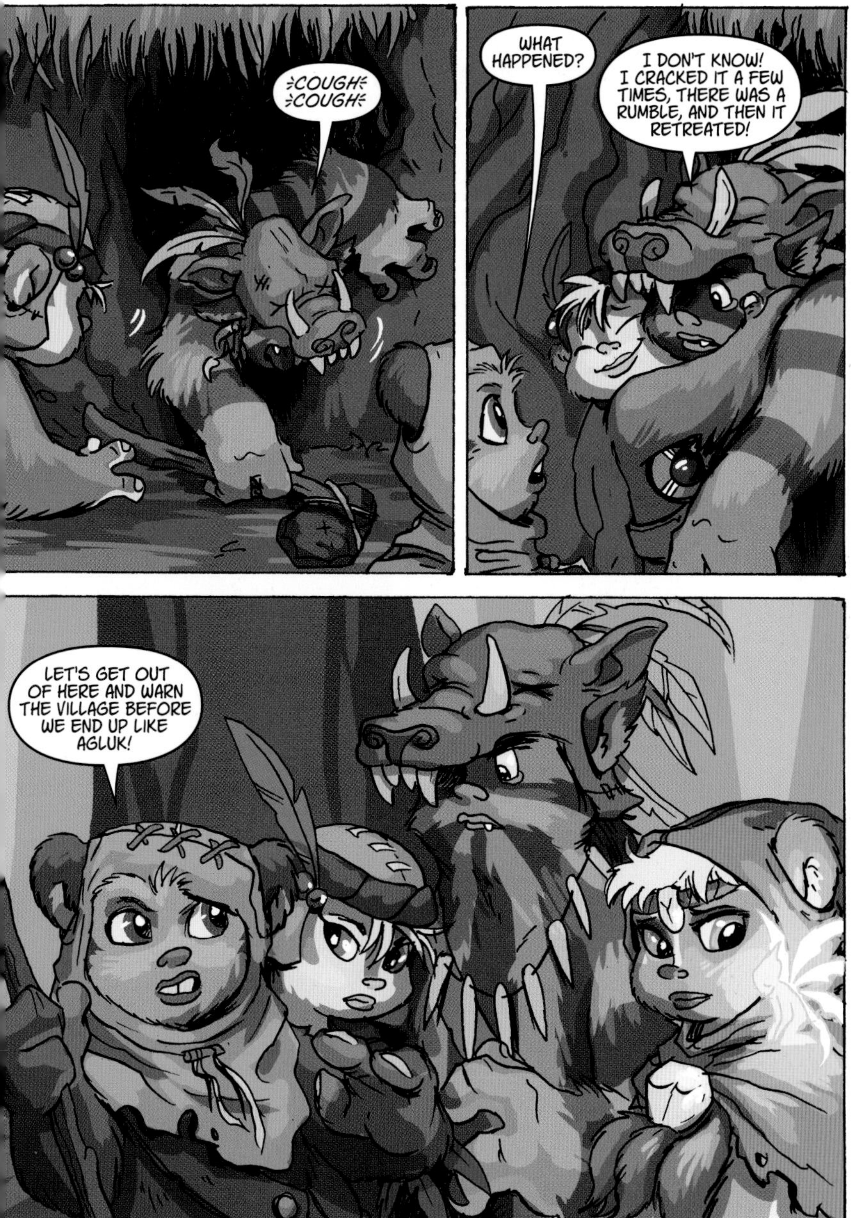

COUGH
COUGH
WHAT HAPPENED?
I DON'T KNOW! I CRACKED IT A FEW TIMES, THERE WAS A RUMBLE, AND THEN IT RETREATED!
LET'S GET OUT OF HERE AND WARN THE VILLAGE BEFORE WE END UP LIKE AGLUK!

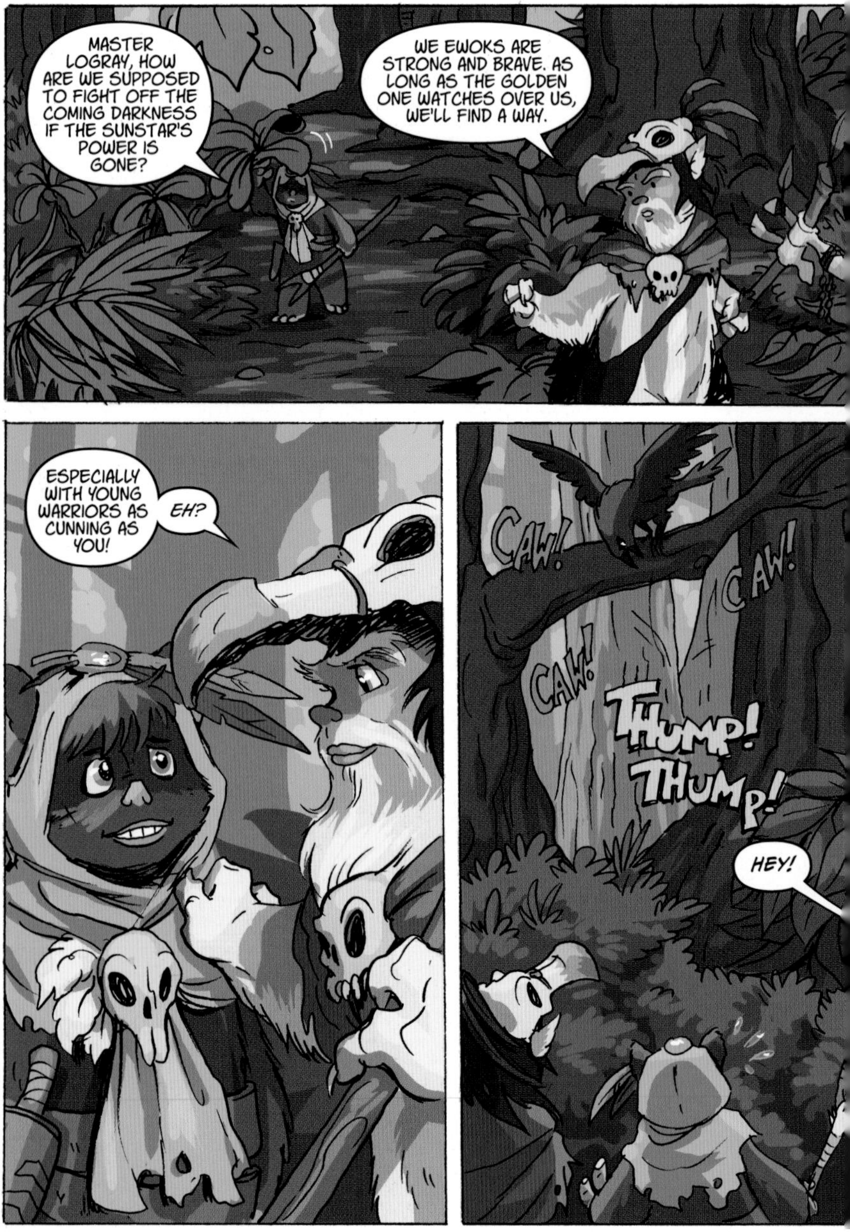
MASTER LOGRAY, HOW ARE WE SUPPOSED TO FIGHT OFF THE COMING DARKNESS IF THE SUNSTAR'S POWER IS GONE?
WE EWOKS ARE STRONG AND BRAVE. AS LONG AS THE GOLDEN ONE WATCHES OVER US, WE'LL FIND A WAY.
ESPECIALLY WITH YOUNG WARRIORS AS CUNNING AS YOU!
EH?
CAW!
CAW!
CAW!
THUMP! THUMP!
HEY!

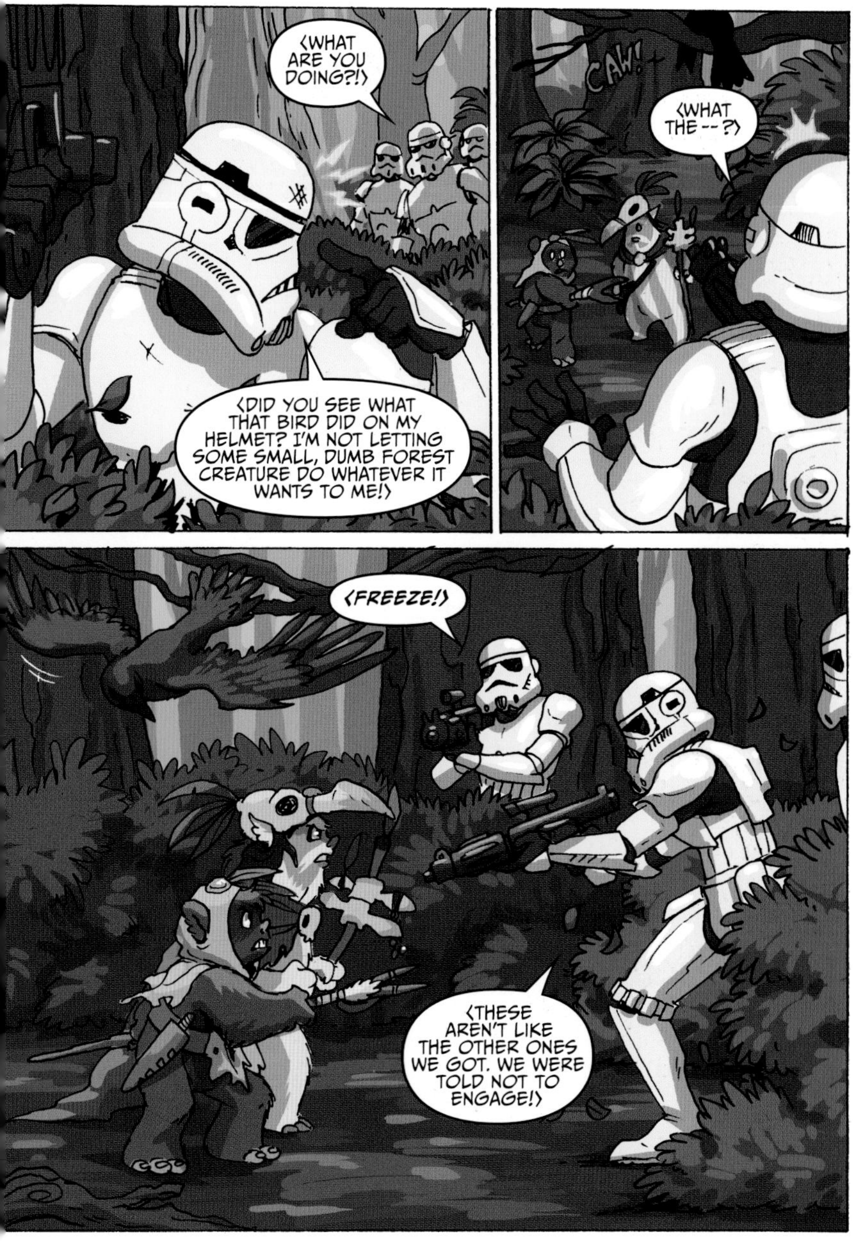
<WHAT ARE YOU DOING?!>
<DID YOU SEE WHAT THAT BIRD DID ON MY HELMET? I'M NOT LETTING SOME SMALL, DUMB FOREST CREATURE DO WHATEVER IT WANTS TO ME!>
CAW!
<WHAT THE --?>
<FREEZE!>
<THESE AREN'T LIKE THE OTHER ONES WE GOT. WE WERE TOLD NOT TO ENGAGE!>

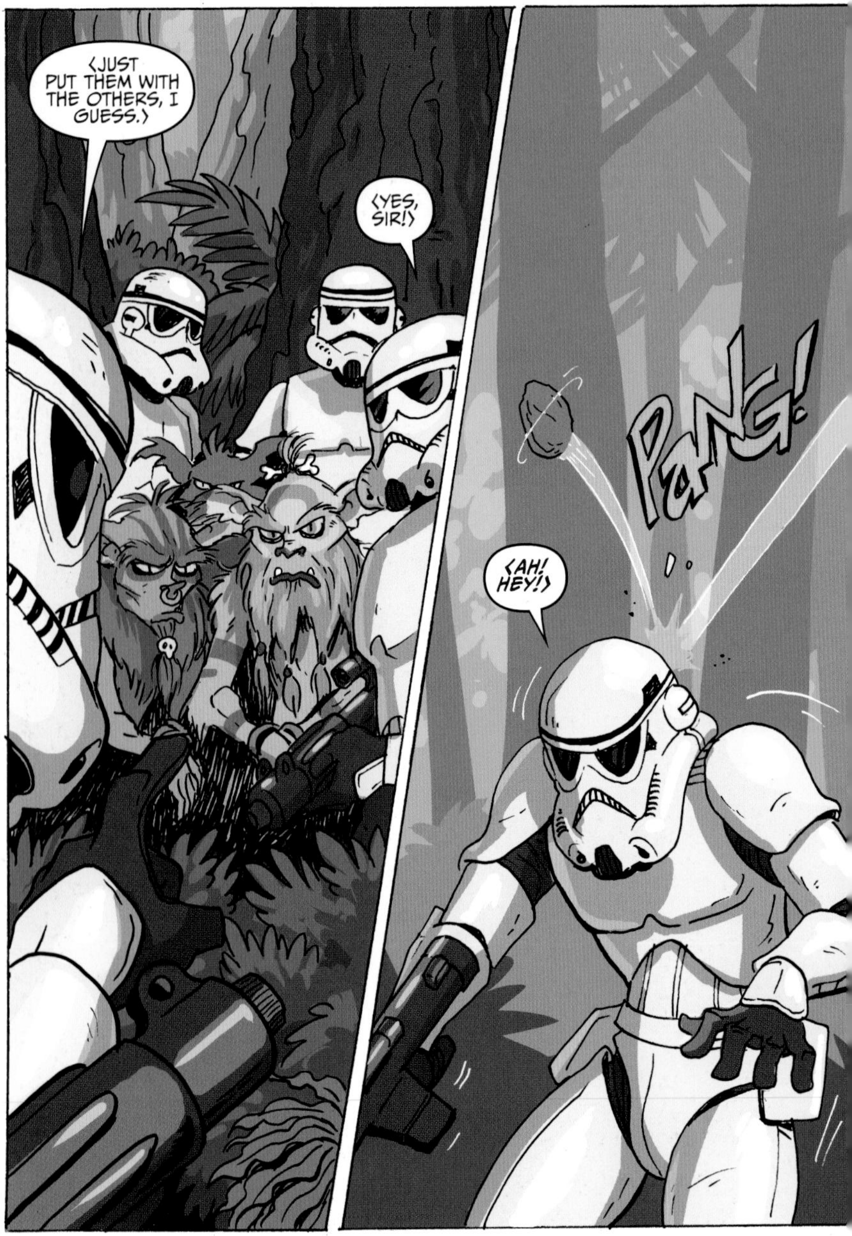
<JUST PUT THEM WITH THE OTHERS, I GUESS.>
<YES, SIR!>
PANG!
<AH! HEY!>

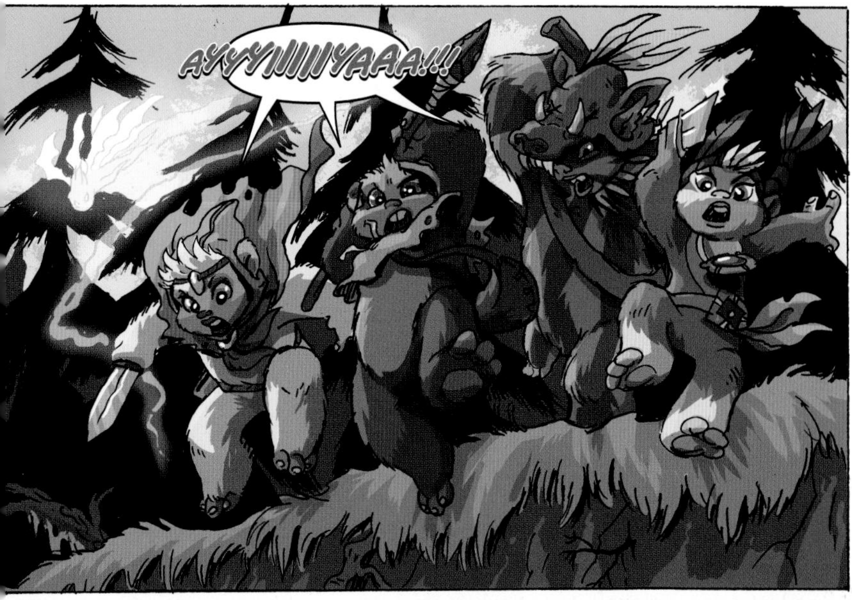
AYYYIIIIIIYAAA!!!

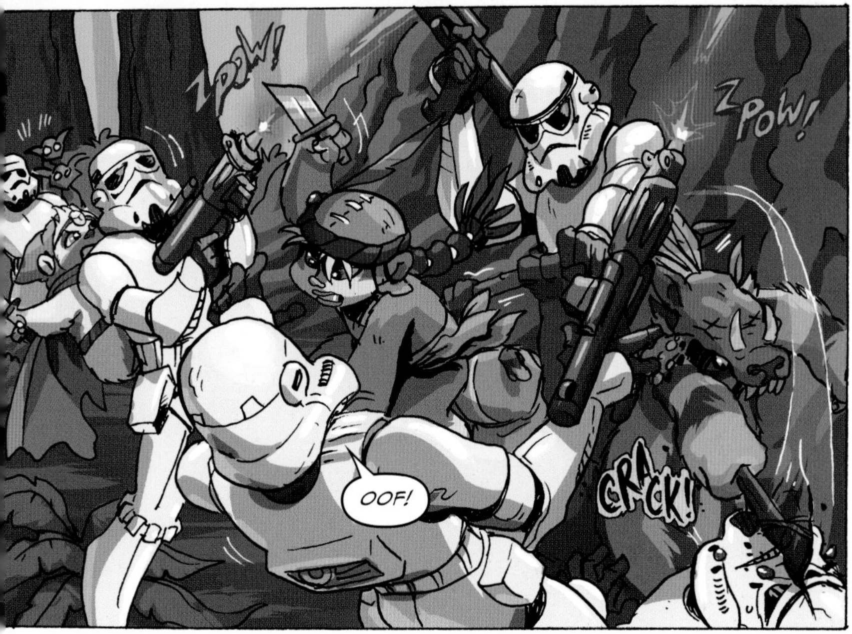
ZPOW!
ZPOW!
OOF!
CRACK!

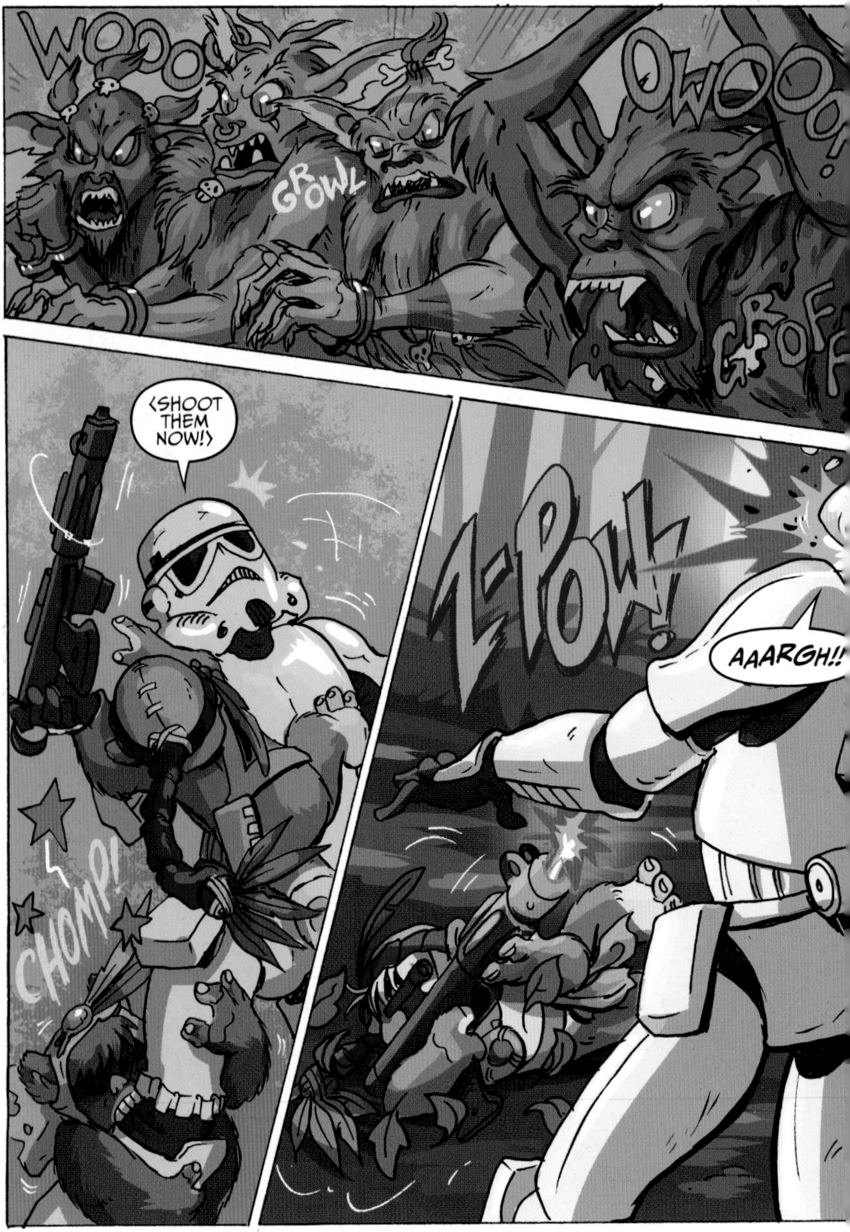

WOOOO
GROWL
OWOOOO!
GROFF
<SHOOT THEM NOW!>
CHOMP!
Z-POW!
AAARGH!!

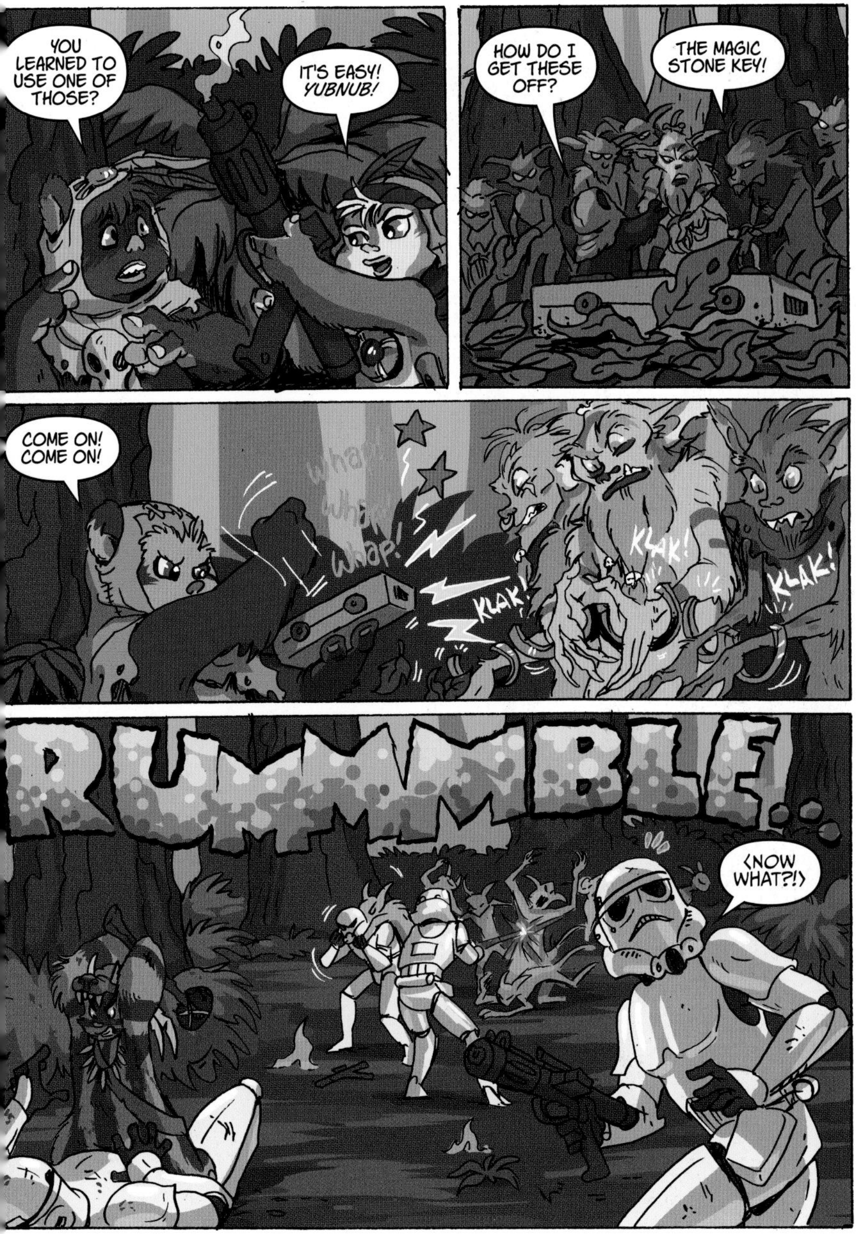
YOU LEARNED TO USE ONE OF THOSE?
IT'S EASY! *YUBNUB!*
HOW DO I GET THESE OFF?
THE MAGIC STONE KEY!
COME ON! COME ON!
KLAK!
KLAK!
KLAK!
RUMMBLE...
<NOW WHAT?!>

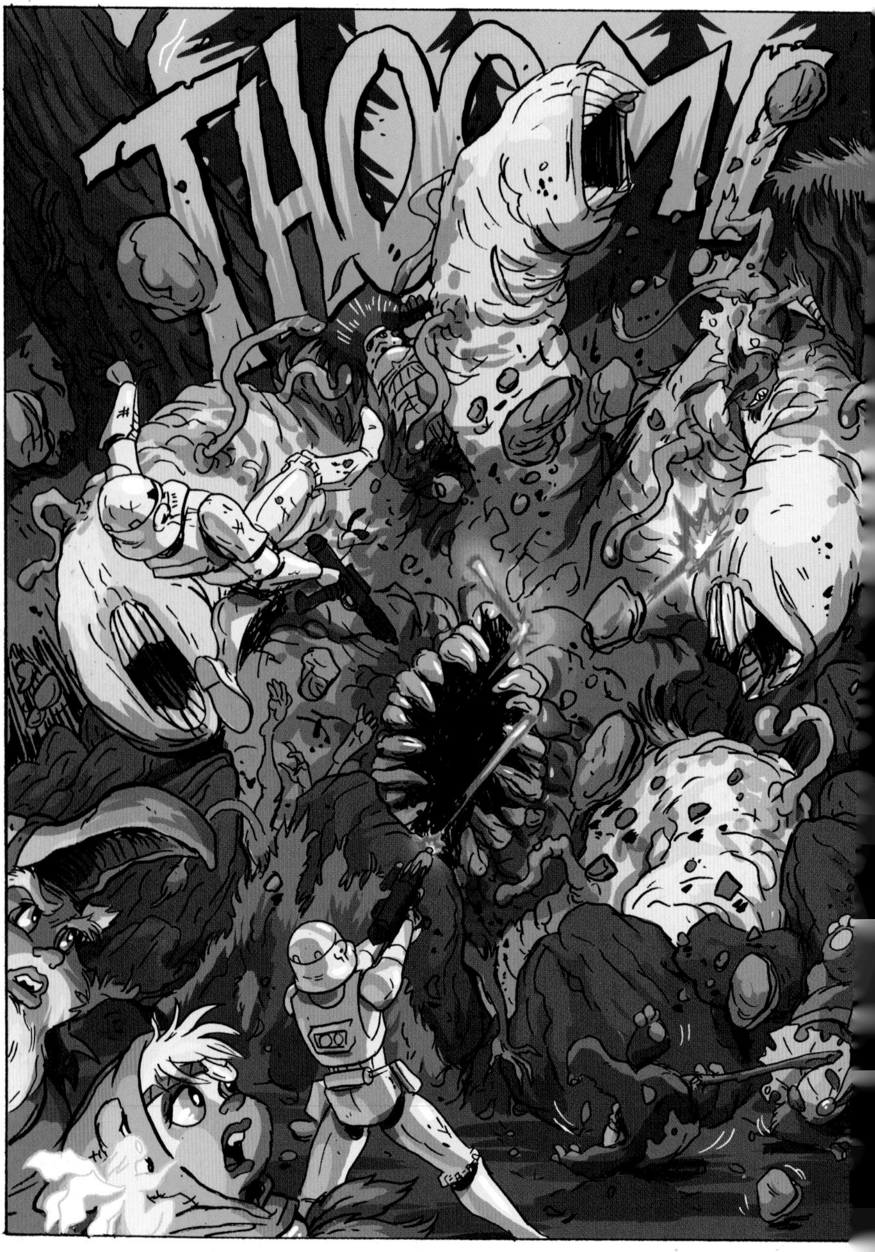
THOOM!

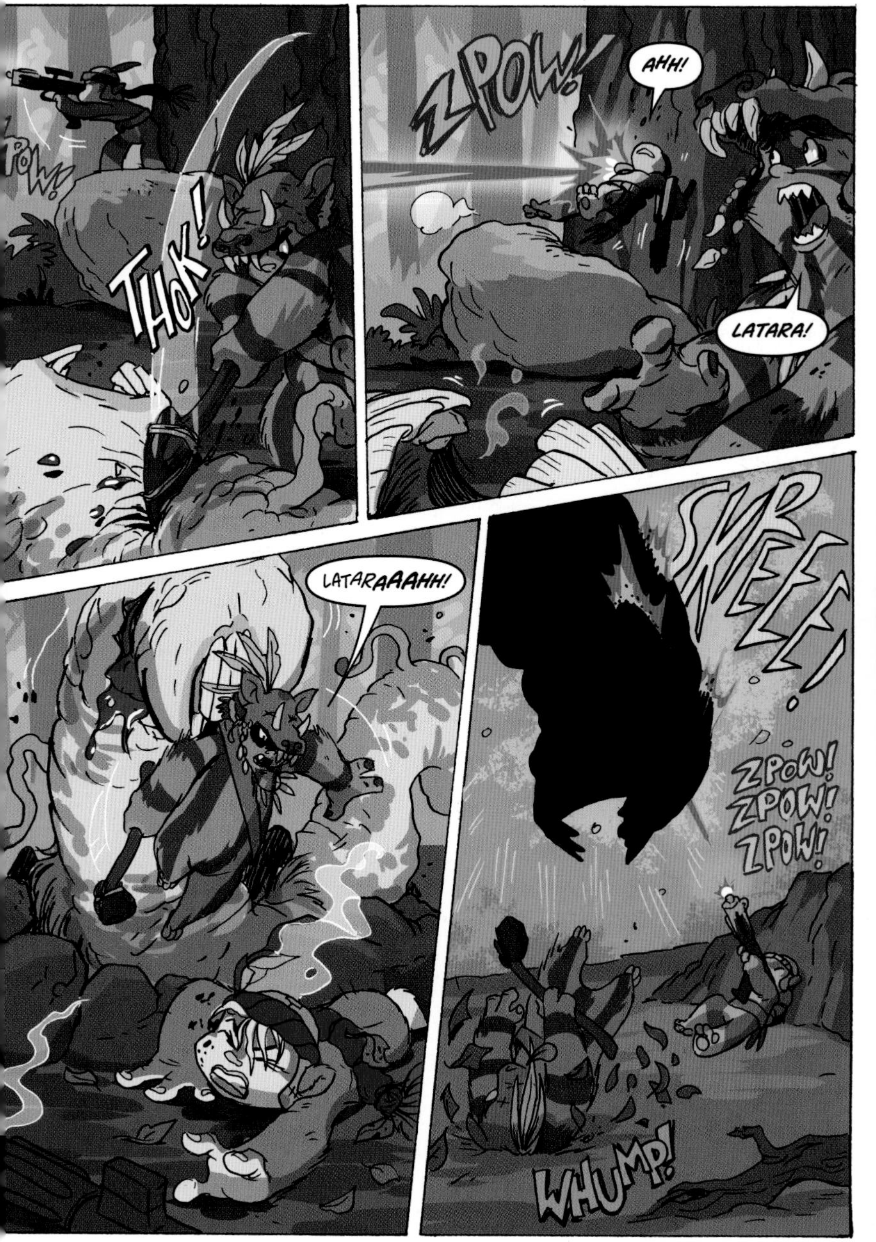
POW!
THOK!
ZPOW!
AHH!
LATARA!
LATARAAAHH!
SWEEEE!
ZPOW!
ZPOW!
ZPOW!
WHUMP!

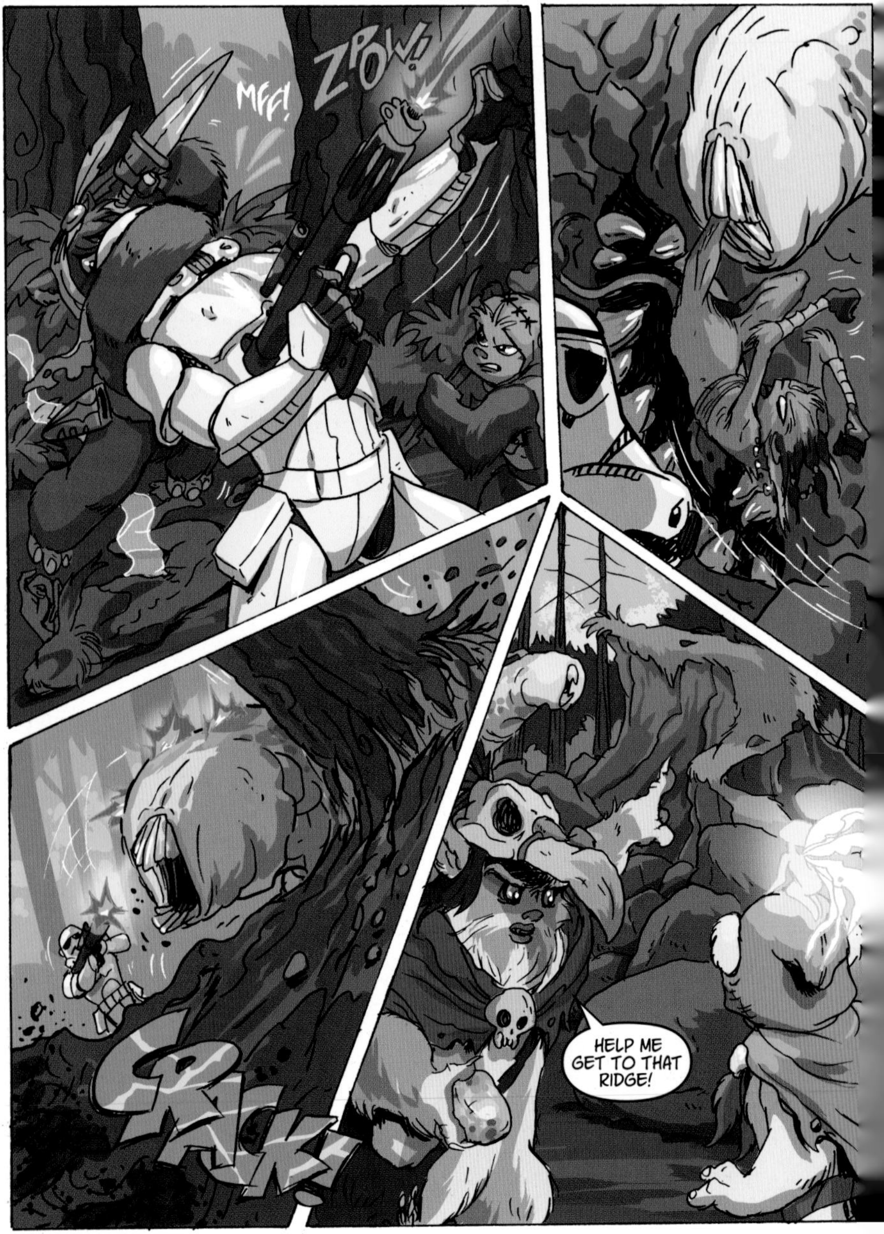
ZPOW!
MFF!
HELP ME GET TO THAT RIDGE!

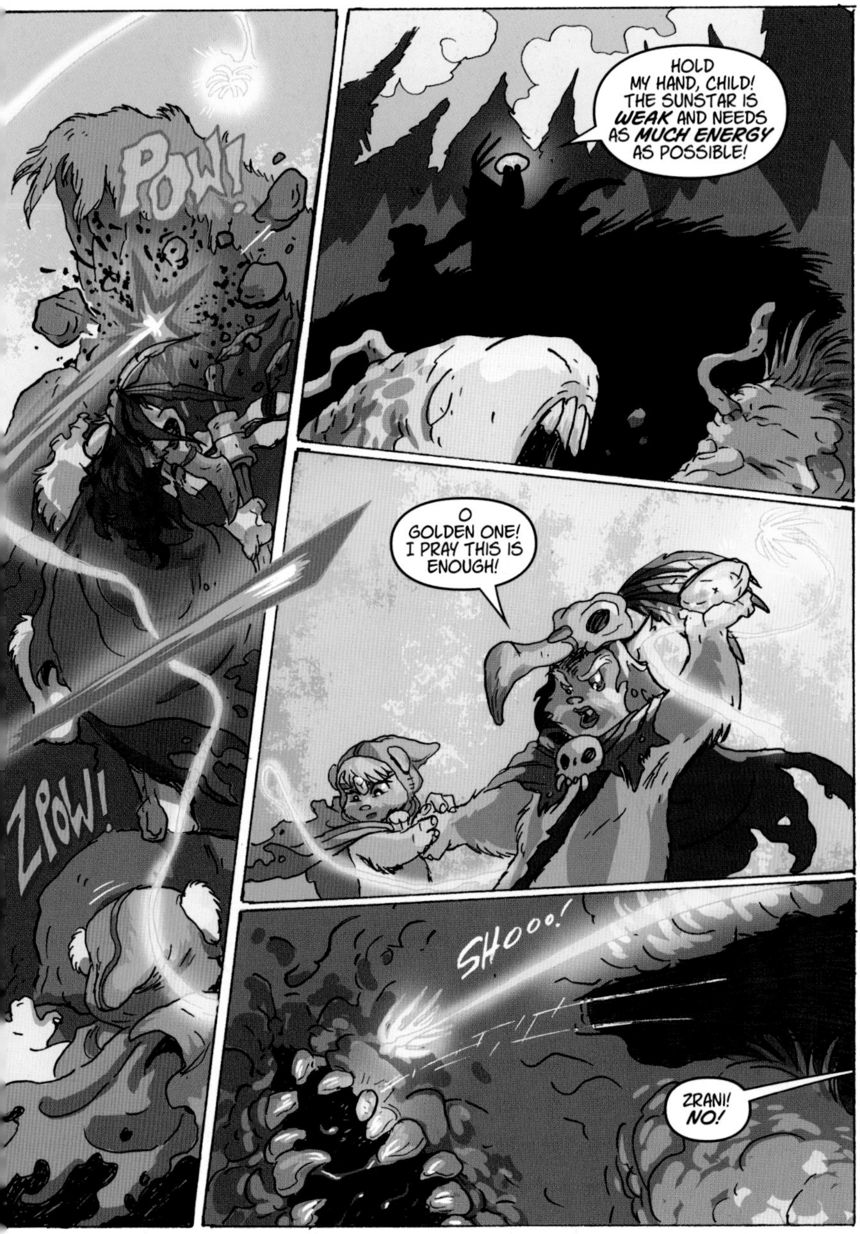
POW!
HOLD MY HAND, CHILD! THE SUNSTAR IS WEAK AND NEEDS AS MUCH ENERGY AS POSSIBLE!
ZPOW!
O GOLDEN ONE! I PRAY THIS IS ENOUGH!
SHOOO!
ZRANI! NO!

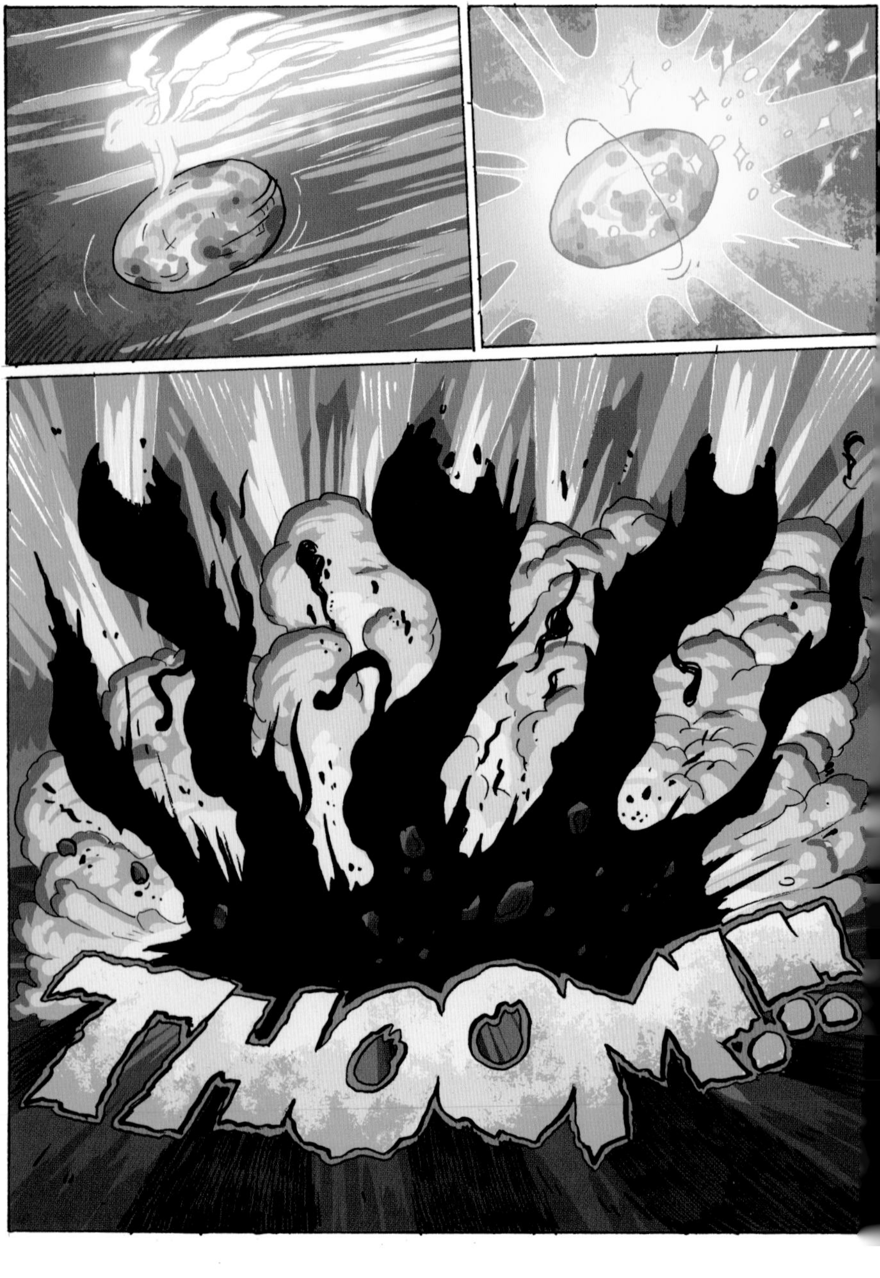
THOOM!!

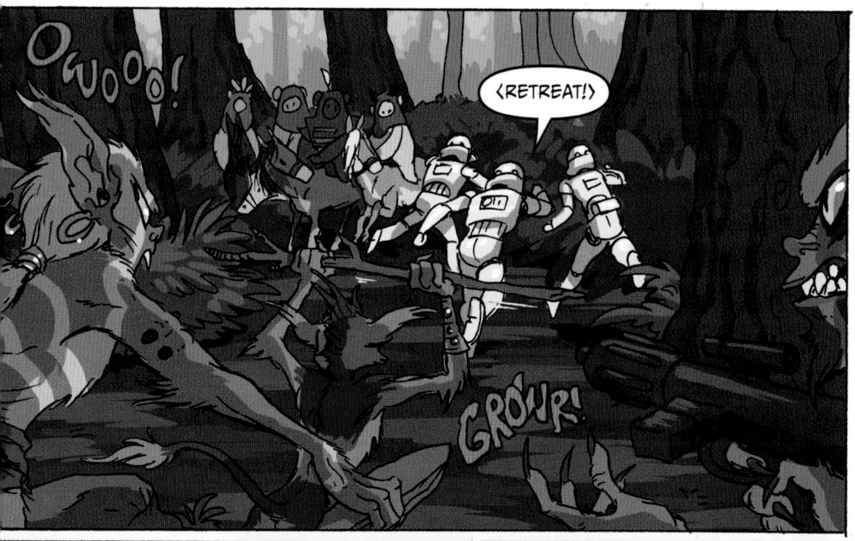
OWOOO!
⟨RETREAT!⟩
GROWR!

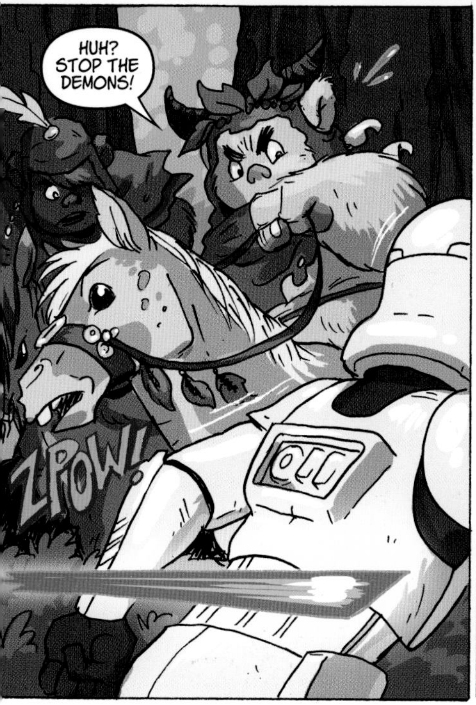
HUH? STOP THE DEMONS!
ZPOW!

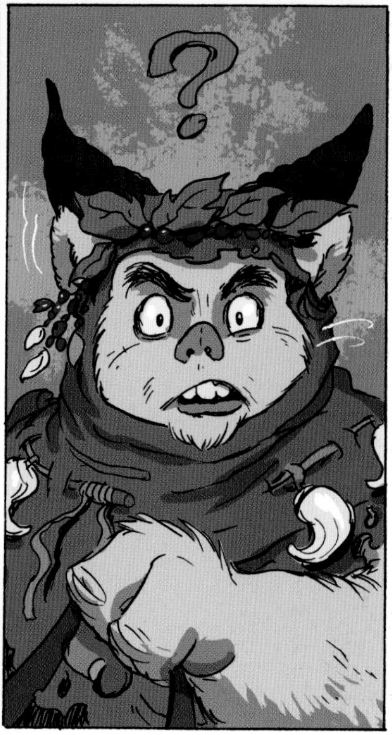
?

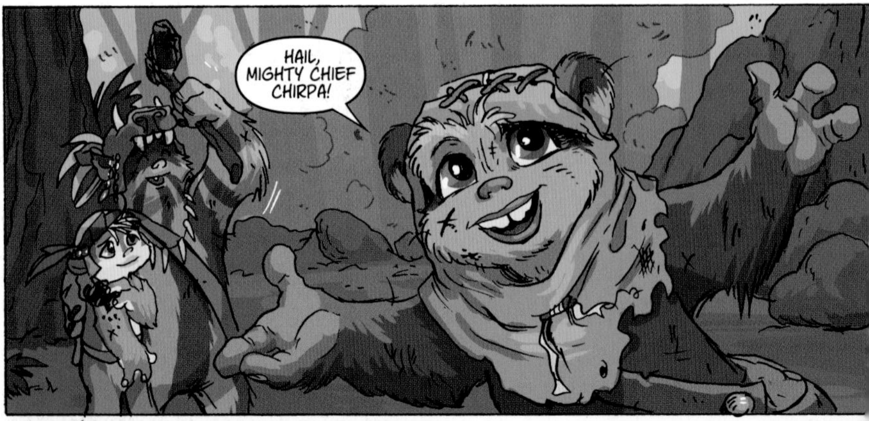
HAIL, MIGHTY CHIEF CHIRPA!

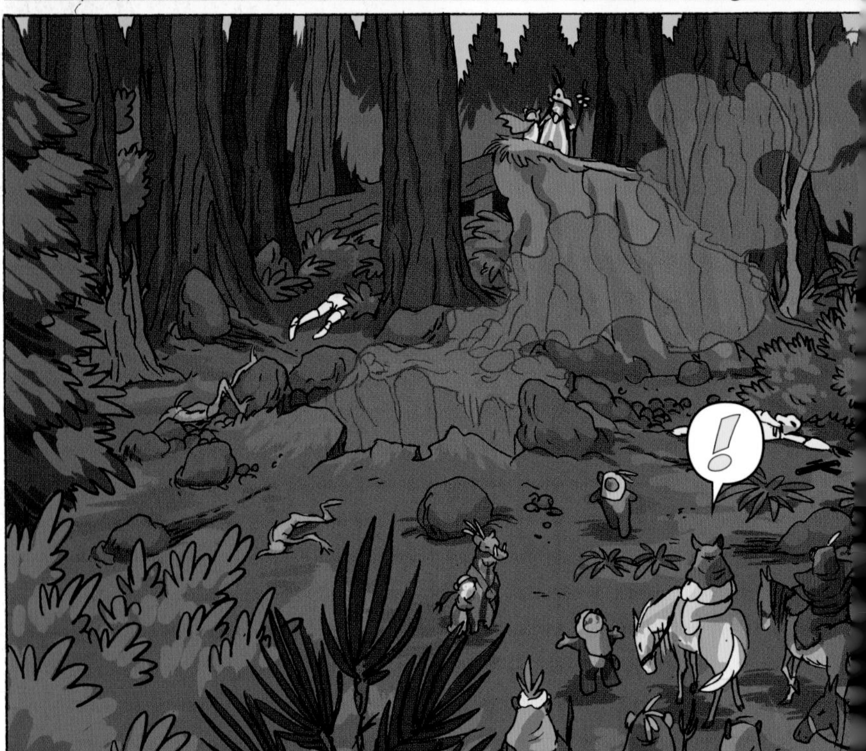
!

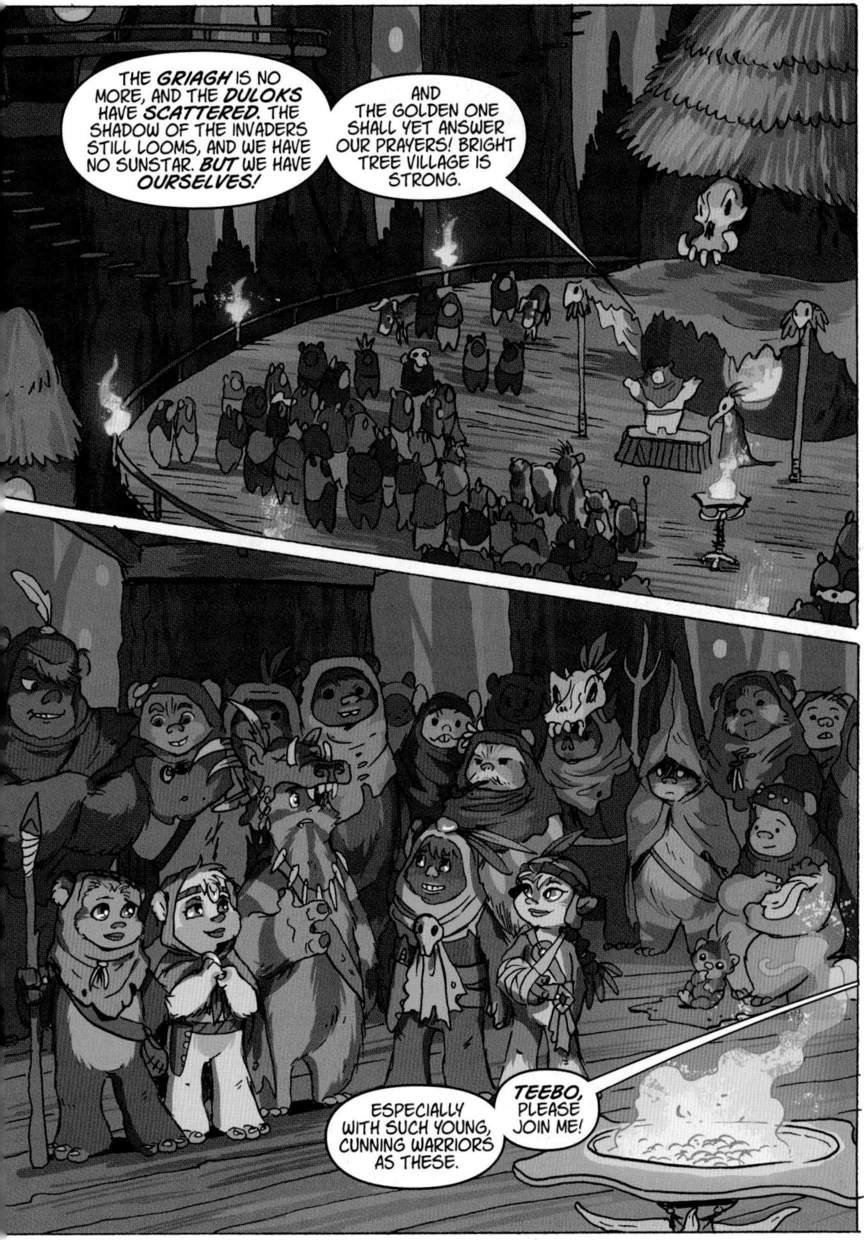
THE GRIAGH IS NO MORE, AND THE DULOKS HAVE SCATTERED. THE SHADOW OF THE INVADERS STILL LOOMS, AND WE HAVE NO SUNSTAR. BUT WE HAVE OURSELVES!
AND THE GOLDEN ONE SHALL YET ANSWER OUR PRAYERS! BRIGHT TREE VILLAGE IS STRONG.
ESPECIALLY WITH SUCH YOUNG, CUNNING WARRIORS AS THESE.
TEEBO, PLEASE JOIN ME!

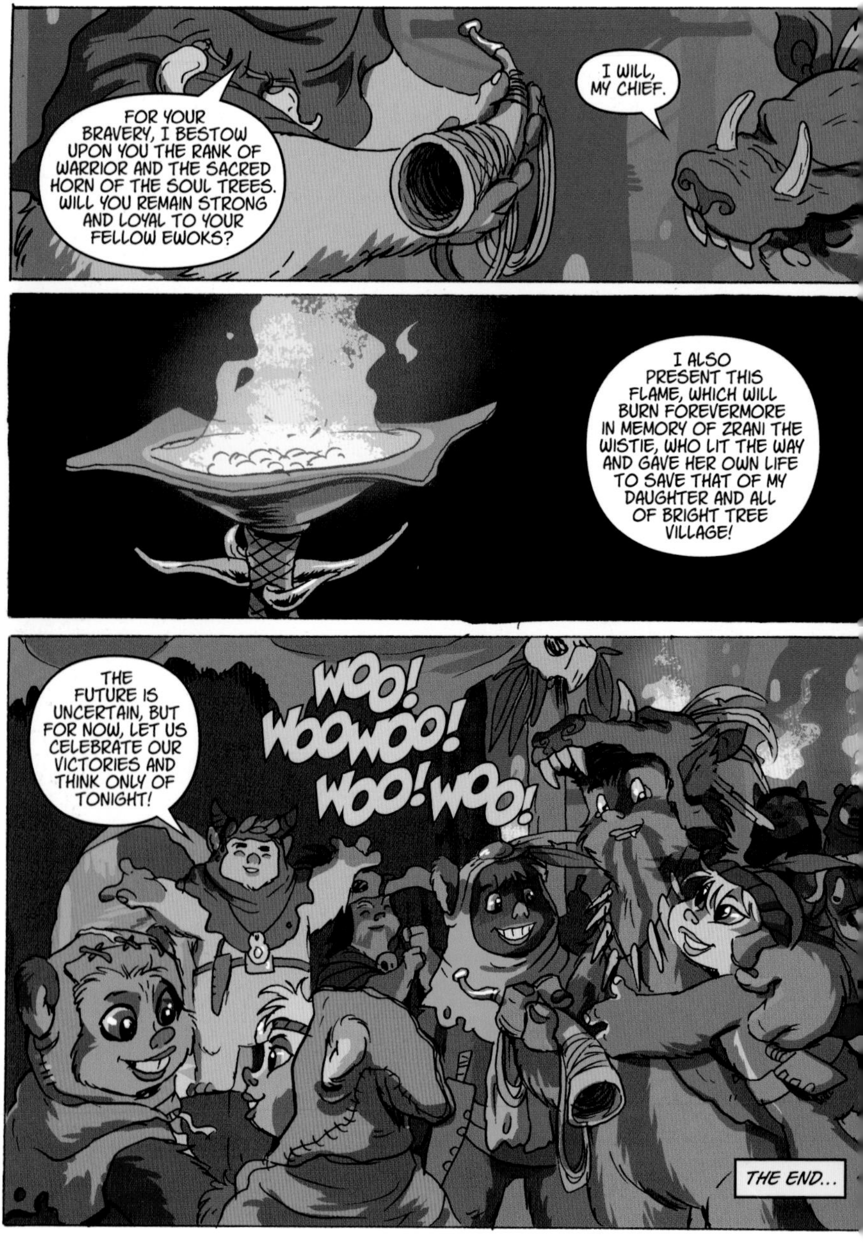
FOR YOUR BRAVERY, I BESTOW UPON YOU THE RANK OF WARRIOR AND THE SACRED HORN OF THE SOUL TREES. WILL YOU REMAIN STRONG AND LOYAL TO YOUR FELLOW EWOKS?
I WILL, MY CHIEF.
I ALSO PRESENT THIS FLAME, WHICH WILL BURN FOREVERMORE IN MEMORY OF ZRANI THE WISTIE, WHO LIT THE WAY AND GAVE HER OWN LIFE TO SAVE THAT OF MY DAUGHTER AND ALL OF BRIGHT TREE VILLAGE!
THE FUTURE IS UNCERTAIN, BUT FOR NOW, LET US CELEBRATE OUR VICTORIES AND THINK ONLY OF TONIGHT!
WOO! WOOWOO! WOO! WOO!
THE END...

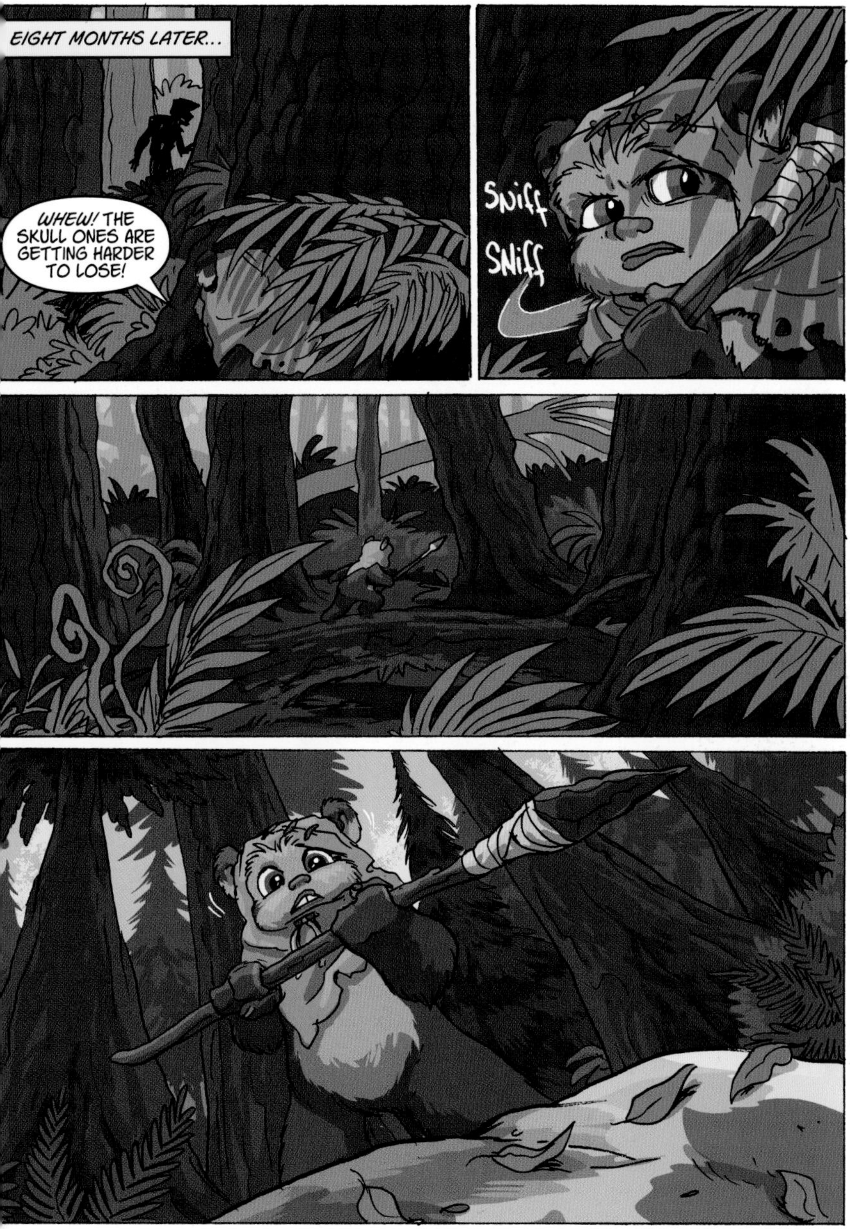
EIGHT MONTHS LATER...
WHEW! THE SKULL ONES ARE GETTING HARDER TO LOSE!
SNIFF
SNIFF

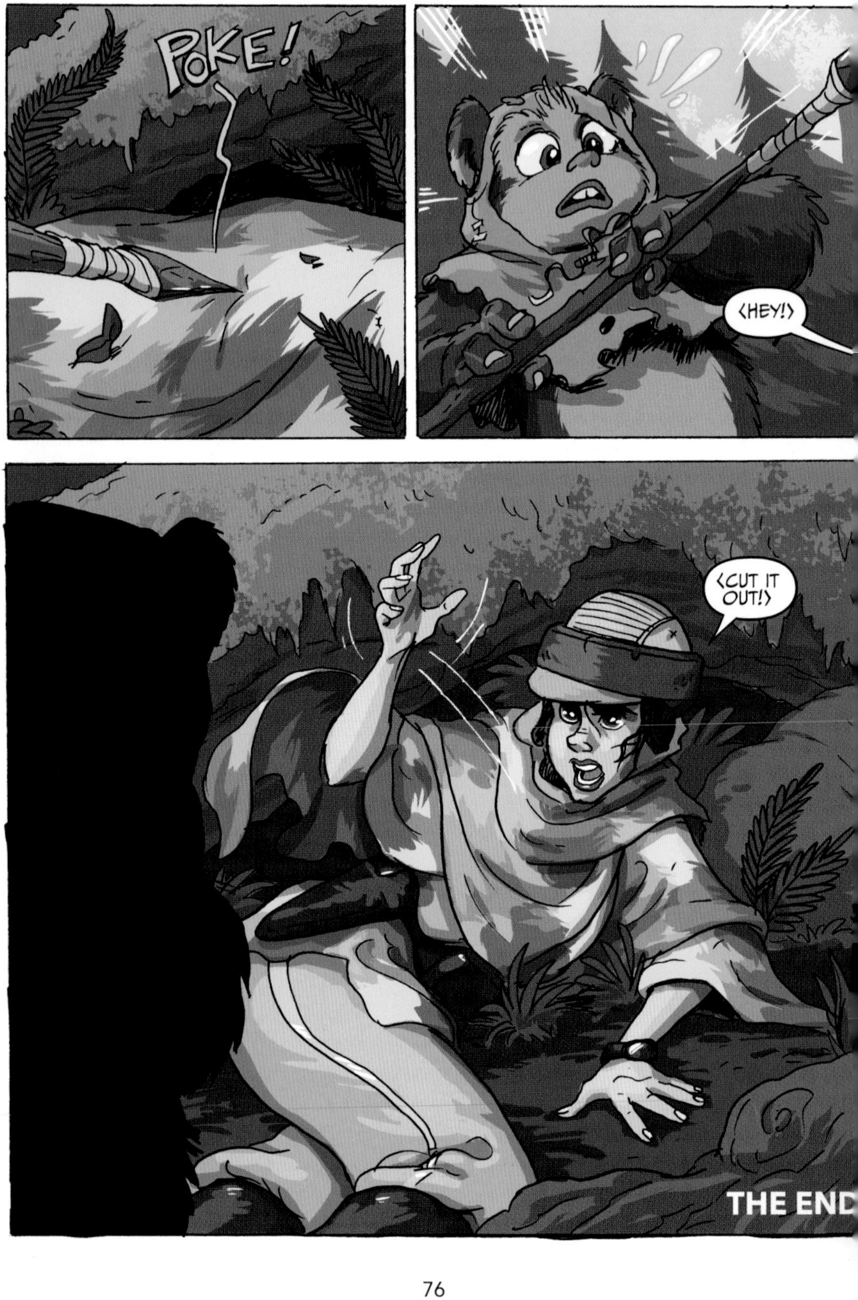
POKE!
<HEY!>
<CUT IT OUT!>
THE END

EXECUTIVE VICE PRESIDENT NEIL HANKERSON
CHIEF FINANCIAL OFFICER TOM WEDDLE
VICE PRESIDENT OF PUBLISHING RANDY STRADLEY
VICE PRESIDENT OF BOOK TRADE SALES MICHAEL MARTENS
VICE PRESIDENT OF BUSINESS AFFAIRS ANITA NELSON
EDITOR IN CHIEF SCOTT ALLIE
VICE PRESIDENT OF MARKETING MATT PARKINSON
VICE PRESIDENT OF PRODUCT DEVELOPMENT DAVID SCROGGY
VICE PRESIDENT OF INFORMATION TECHNOLOGY DALE LAFOUNTAIN
SENIOR DIRECTOR OF PRINT, DESIGN, AND PRODUCTION DARLENE VOGEL
GENERAL COUNSEL KEN LIZZI
EDITORIAL DIRECTOR DAVEY ESTRADA
SENIOR BOOKS EDITOR CHRIS WARNER
EXECUTIVE EDITOR DIANA SCHUTZ
DIRECTOR OF PRINT AND DEVELOPMENT CARY GRAZZINI
ART DIRECTOR LIA RIBACCHI
DIRECTOR OF SCHEDULING CARA NIECE
DIRECTOR OF INTERNATIONAL LICENSING TIM WIESCH
DIRECTOR OF DIGITAL PUBLISHING MARK BERNARDI

STAR WARS GRAPHIC NOVEL TIMELINE (IN YEARS)

Dawn of the Jedi—36,000 BSW4
Omnibus: Tales of the Jedi—5,000–3,986 BSW4
Knights of the Old Republic—3,964–3,963 BSW4
The Old Republic—3678, 3653, 3600 BSW4
Lost Tribe of the Sith—2974 BSW4
Knight Errant—1,032 BSW4
Jedi vs. Sith—1,000 BSW4
Jedi: The Dark Side—53 BSW4
Omnibus: Rise of the Sith—33 BSW4
Episode I: The Phantom Menace—32 BSW4
Omnibus: Emissaries and Assassins—32 BSW4
Omnibus: Quinlan Vos—Jedi in Darkness—31–30 BSW4
Omnibus: Menace Revealed—31–22 BSW4
Honor and Duty—22 BSW4
Blood Ties—22 BSW4
Episode II: Attack of the Clones—22 BSW4
Clone Wars—22–19 BSW4
Omnibus: Clone Wars—22–19 BSW4
Clone Wars Adventures—22–19 BSW4
Darth Maul: Death Sentence—20 BSW4
Episode III: Revenge of the Sith—19 BSW4
Purge—19 BSW4
Dark Times—19 BSW4
Omnibus: Droids and Ewoks—15 BSW4–3.5 ASW4
Omnibus: Droids—5.5 BSW4
Omnibus: Boba Fett—3 BSW4–10 ASW4
Agent of the Empire—3 BSW4
The Force Unleashed—2 BSW4
Omnibus: At War with the Empire—1 BSW4
Episode IV: A New Hope—SW4
Star Wars—0 ASW4
Classic Star Wars—0–3 ASW4
Omnibus: A Long Time Ago. . . .—0–4 ASW4
Omnibus: Wild Space—0–4 ASW4
Empire—0 ASW4
Omnibus: The Other Sons of Tatooine—0 ASW4
Omnibus: Early Victories—0–3 ASW4
Jabba the Hutt: The Art of the Deal—1 ASW4
Episode V: The Empire Strikes Back—3 ASW4
Omnibus: Shadows of the Empire—3.5–4.5 ASW4
Episode VI: Return of the Jedi—4 ASW4
Omnibus: X-Wing Rogue Squadron—4–5 ASW4
The Thrawn Trilogy—9 ASW4
Dark Empire—10 ASW4
Crimson Empire—11 ASW4
Jedi Academy: Leviathan—12 ASW4
Union—19 ASW4
Chewbacca—25 ASW4
Invasion—25 ASW4
Legacy—130–138 ASW4

Dawn of the Jedi
36,000 years before
Star Wars: A New Hope

Old Republic Era
25,000–1000 years before
Star Wars: A New Hope

Rise of the Empire Era
1000–0 years before Star
Wars: A New Hope

Rebellion Era
0–5 years after
Star Wars: A New Hope

New Republic Era
5–25 years after
Star Wars: A New Hope

New Jedi Order Era
25+ years after
Star Wars: A New Hope

Legacy Era
130+ years after
Star Wars: A New Hope

Vector
Crosses four eras in timeline

Volume 1 contains:
Knights of the Old Republic Volume
Dark Times Volume 3
Volume 2 contains:
Rebellion Volume 4
Legacy Volume 6

Infinities
Does not apply to timeline

Sergio Aragones Stomps Star Wars
Star Wars Tales
Omnibus: Infinities
Tag and Bink
Star Wars Visionaries

BSW4 = before *Episode IV: A New Hope*. ASW4 = after *Episode IV: A New Hope*.

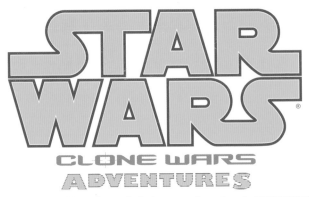

STAR WARS®

CLONE WARS ADVENTURES

Don't miss any of the action-packed adventures of your favorite STAR WARS® characters, available at comics shops and bookstores in a galaxy near you!

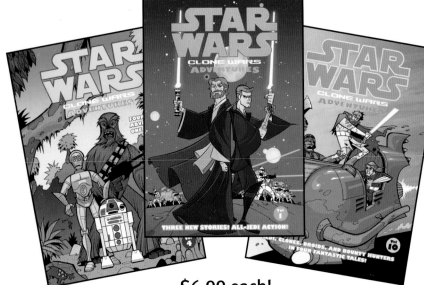

STAR WARS
CLONE WARS
ADVENTURES
Vol 4
STAR WARS
CLONE WARS
ADVENTURES
Vol 1
THREE NEW STORIES! ALL-JEDI ACTION!
STAR WARS
CLONE WARS
ADVENTURES
Vol 10
EDI, CLONES, DROIDS, AND BOUNTY HUNTERS IN FOUR FANTASTIC TALES!

$6.99 each!

Volume 1 ISBN 978-1-59307-243-8	**Volume 2** ISBN 978-1-59307-271-1	**Volume 3** ISBN 978-1-59307-307-7	**Volume 4** ISBN 978-1-59307-402-9	**Volume 5** ISBN 978-1-59307-4
Volume 6 ISBN 978-1-59307-567-5	**Volume 7** ISBN 978-1-59307-678-8	**Volume 8** ISBN 978-1-59307-680-1	**Volume 9** ISBN 978-1-59307-832-4	**Volume 10** ISBN 978-1-59307-8

AVAILABLE AT YOUR LOCAL COMICS SHOP OR BOOKSTORE

To find a comics shop in your area, call 1-888-266-4226

For more information or to order direct: • On the web: darkhorse.com • Phone: 1-800-862-0052 Mon.–Fri. 9 AM to 5 PM Pacific Time • E-mail: mailorder@darkhorse.com *Prices and availability subject to change without notice.